"Mark Yarhouse has written a soli... biblically grounded, and conceptu... with youth and young adults grappling with issues of sexuality and sexual identity. It is precisely the kind of book that I would expect from someone who exemplifies irenic engagement around these conflictual issues in the professional and academic worlds in a way that is simultaneously distinctively Christian, winsome, and intellectually elegant. I recommend this book highly."

Stanton L. Jones, PhD, coauthor of the *God's Design for Sex* family sex education book series

"With the gentleness of a father, the expertise of a scholar, and the compassion of one who has ministered to youth and their families, Mark Yarhouse invites us into a candid conversation about some of the most challenging questions facing youth and families in the church—those of sexuality and gender. For over a decade, Mark has been at the forefront of evangelical scholarship on issues of sexuality. His research has led to new understandings about the way sexual identity is formed as children grow into adulthood. In this book he makes that research accessible to youth pastors and families, introducing the most important questions at the heart of sexuality. If these questions matter to you, your family, your youth group, or your church, you need to read this book."

Barrett McRay, PsyD, Chair of Christian Formation and Ministry at Wheaton College

MARK A. YARHOUSE

FOREWORD BY
WESLEY HILL

UNDER STANDING SEXUAL IDENTITY

A RESOURCE FOR **YOUTH MINISTRY**

youth
specialties

ZONDERVAN

Understanding Sexual Identity: A Resource for Youth Ministry
Copyright © 2013 by Mark A. Yarhouse

This title is also available as a Zondervan ebook.
Visit www.zondervan.com/ebooks.

Requests for information should be addressed to:

Zondervan, *Grand Rapids, Michigan 49530*

Library of Congress Cataloging-in-Publication Data

Yarhouse, Mark A., 1968–
        Understanding sexual identity : a resource for youth ministry /
Mark Yarhouse.
            pages cm
        Includes bibliographical references.
        ISBN 978-0-310-51618-7 (softcover)
        1. Church work with youth. 2. Church work with teenagers. 3. Gender identity. 4. Sex—Religious aspects—Christianity. 5. Identity (Psychology)— Religious aspects—Christianity. I. Title.
        BV4447.Y37—2013
        261.8'3576—dc23   2013024800

All Scripture quotations, unless otherwise indicated, are taken from The Holy Bible, *New International Version®, NIV®.* Copyright © 2011 by Biblica, Inc.™ Used by permission. All rights reserved worldwide.

Cover design: Micah Kandros
Cover photography: © Edyta Pawlowska/Shutterstock
Interior design: David Conn and Ben Fetterley
Interior Photography: David Schliepp/www.123RF.com; dervish37/www.123RF.com; Yulia Glam/www.123RF.com; Paula Stephens/www.123RF.com

Printed in the United States of America

14 15 16 /DCI/ 20 19 18 17 16 15 14 13 12 11 10 9 8 7 6 5 4 3 2

CONTENTS

FOREWORD

WHEN I WAS 11 OR 12 AND TRANSITIONING FROM THE children's ministry into the youth group, I was awakening to the fact that I was attracted to guys, not girls.

That realization terrified me. What did it mean?

A few months earlier, my parents had given me a copy of a popular guide to navigating adolescence. In that book, I had read: "Homosexuality is an abnormal desire that reflects deep problems, but it doesn't happen very often, and it's not likely to happen to you."*

But it *was* happening to me. Did that mean I was a person with "deep problems"? Did that mean I was "abnormal"? And if so, what should I do about that?

Other voices I heard—for instance, the Christian radio talk show hosts I listened to occasionally as I rode in the car with my parents—said that many Christian teenagers experience homosexuality as a "phase." "Don't worry," these voices seemed to say. "You'll outgrow your same-sex attraction, just like kids outgrow their obsession with certain childhood toys."

---

* James Dobson, *Preparing for Adolescence* (Ventura, CA: Gospel Light, 2005 [1992]), p. 71.

But as I continued to mature, I didn't seem to be outgrowing my desires. If anything, those attractions seemed to be getting stronger. In the midst of all this questioning and confusion, I stayed involved in my church's youth group. I participated in Bible studies. I attended summer camps. I volunteered in service projects and mission efforts. I went out for lunch regularly with my youth pastor and talked about how the Christian gospel was meant to inform and direct my daily life. Sadly, though, I didn't feel, in any of these settings, that I could be honest about my sexuality.

I now wonder why I felt the need for secrecy. My youth pastor was wise and kind and compassionate. In many ways, he was an exemplary leader who wanted nothing more than to help us all grow and flourish in our faith. But I think I also sensed, even at that young age, that he wasn't equipped to respond well if I had admitted, "I think I'm gay."

I was afraid that if I told him, he would immediately suggest I see a therapist and try to "change" and become straight. And I feared that response—not because I was convinced that "change" was impossible, but because it didn't seem like a response that was sensitive to the particular, irreducible shape of my unique life story. I was afraid of being put into a neat category or offered a simple, tidy solution. Already, as a young teenager, I knew that there *were* no simple solutions. And I wanted to talk with a youth pastor who knew that, too.

Mark Yarhouse has written a book that describes, better than almost anything I've read, the kinds of questions I was asking when I was a teenager in my church's youth group—and a book that, in turn, gives youth pastors the necessary tools to engage those questions with delicacy, discernment, faithfulness, and love.

In the pages that follow you'll gain insight into how young people try to construct a sexual identity for themselves. You'll learn about the "scripts"—explicit and implicit—that your church, and the surrounding culture, are offering sexual minorities in that process. And you'll learn much else besides. Most of all, you'll receive a glimpse into what it might look like to be a person of safety and refuge for the young people to whom you minister.

If we all took to heart the instructions in this book, our churches would be more characterized by the grace and mercy of Christ. And kids like the one I used to be would stand a greater chance of finding youth leaders who could introduce them to that grace and mercy for themselves.

—Wesley Hill, author of *Washed and Waiting: Reflections on Christian Faithfulness and Homosexuality*

PREFACE

THE ILLINOIS PRAIRIE PATH ENCOMPASSES OVER 60 miles of walking and biking paths that course through sections of DuPage, Kane, and Cook Counties. When we lived in Wheaton and later in Glen Ellyn, Illinois, my wife and I often enjoyed biking on the Prairie Path. In fact, I remember walking with her on the day we decided to go back to graduate school. I had just completed my master's in clinical psychology, and we had been praying about whether to return to complete the doctorate. One of the considerations: We had delayed ministry for the past two years while I was in graduate school. During those years, we just went to Sunday morning services; that was about all we could manage. We were looking at several more years of education, and neither of us felt we could put off ministry in the local church for another five years. When we decided together to continue down the path of more school, we also decided to serve our local church as volunteers with the high school youth group. Over the course of the next four years, we had our share of lock-ins, games of "bigger and better," and retreats. Did we "suffer for Jesus" when we took them to Orlando for the Fun in the Son Conference? Sure. You bet. Those were great years, and we fondly recall meeting with our kids on Wednesday mornings for prayer before they would go off to school. They were a great group, and we learned a lot by serving them, their families, and working with great staff, particularly Jean DeVaty, who really did all of the heavy lifting during our time there.

Much has changed in the 15 years or so since we served in youth ministry. I have been conducting research on sexual identity, which refers to the act of labeling oneself based on one's sexual feelings. I've been studying how sexual identity develops over time and what it means to synthesize or achieve a sexual identity as a gay or lesbian person, for example. It has been particularly interesting to consider the role of attributions in sexual-identity development (or how people explain the causes, meaning, and purpose of their same-sex sexuality), particularly among Christians who experience same-sex attraction.

Most of my recent work has been with Christian colleges and universities. I spoke recently at the Council for Christian Colleges and Universities (CCCU) and have been a resource to that group over the years. My research institute has conducted several studies that have furthered our understanding of college-age students—Christians who are navigating sexual-identity questions. These interviews and surveys often ask about experiences in childhood and adolescence, which makes that work relevant to youth ministry.

In 2012 I was asked to give a plenary address at the Association of Youth Ministry Educators in Dallas, Texas. It was at that conference that Mark Matlock heard me speak about sexual-identity development. He connected the dots to what that could mean for youth ministry staff, and he contacted me that day to see if I could speak the following year at the Youth Specialties National Conferences in San Diego and Nashville.

In preparation for those talks, I began reviewing our data on sexual-identity development with an eye for childhood and especially adolescence—to come to a better understanding of what I would want a youth ministry staff member or volunteer to know about sexual identity. This got me thinking back to my own time helping with youth ministry—thinking through what I would have liked to have been aware of, as well as what I think youth ministry staff need to know in light of how our culture has changed. Of course, youth ministry is broader than church-based ministry, including urban parachurch ministries.

The goal of this book, then, is to help youth ministry staff and volunteers understand critical developmental issues so that they are in better positions to provide more relevant ministry and pastoral care to young people who are sorting out sexual-identity questions or concerns.

What are you going to be reading about? I purposefully develop an image I want you to use to help you think about your role in the life of young people who are sorting out sexual-identity questions or concerns. The image is that of young people navigating difficult terrain. You can imagine them hiking a trail or going off-trail or climbing a mountain. The point is that this is not easy terrain for them to cover. It's going to be difficult. They would like your company. They would like the company of friends, family, and their local church, especially you as a youth minister, as they navigate this terrain. I ask you to become a better trail guide so that you can be with them in a more helpful, meaningful way.

To do that there are some critical pieces of information you are going to need. Think of these things as what is in your back-pack: a compass, flint, flashlight, pocketknife, and so on. You are going to want these tools.

So I let you know in chapter 1 how you can be a better trail guide. Then in chapters 2-4 I discuss (1) the conflict that many young people experience between their faith as Christians and their same-sex attractions, (2) the developmental process of identity formation, and (3) the competing perspectives from the mainstream of the gay community and from the local church.

The rest of the book (chapters 5-11) helps you with some of the unique challenges that arise once you understand the conflict, the developmental perspective, and the various pathways. These challenges include addressing the climate in your youth group, helping kids find social support through the development of meaningful relationships, how to help young people grow in their relationships with God, how to develop a ministry focus, and how to respond to and interact with parents around this difficult topic.

ACKNOWLEDGMENTS

THIS BOOK CAME TOGETHER RATHER QUICKLY. I FOUND that a lot of people extended me grace in helping make that happen. Let's start with my family: my wife, Lori, and my children, Lynnea, Peter, and Celia. They saw a lot of Dad, but it was mostly Dad working on his laptop for a few weeks and not much else. They are also showing me firsthand what it means to go through junior high and high school, and sometimes life can be one of the best teachers.

I want to thank Regent University for support I have received over the years to both conduct original research in this controversial area and also for time to travel and consult with various Christian institutions and ministries. I am particularly thankful for the support I've received from Bill Hathaway and Jennifer Ripley, in their roles as Dean and Program Director, respectively. I am grateful for my colleagues in the Doctoral Program in Clinical Psychology and the School of Psychology and Counseling, especially Jim Sells, Olya Zaporozhets, Corné Bekker, Glen Moriarty, LaTrelle Jackson, Linda Baum, Don Walker, Carissa Dwiwardani, and Joe Francis. I am grateful for the assistance I receive from students from the Institute for the Study of Sexual

Identity (ISSI), especially Holly Doolin, Kristina High, Rebecca Thomas, Charity Lane, Melissa Armstrong, Emma Bucher, Tranese Morgan, Ashley Allen, and Justin Sides. Alumni from our program and from ISSI have also influenced my thinking in this area over the years, particularly Erica Tan, Trista Carr, Jill Kays, Stephanie Nowacki-Butzen, Christine Gow, Heidi Jo Erickson, and Katie Maslowe. Mentors, colleagues, and affiliates of ISSI have also offered me tremendous support and encouragement. They include Stan Jones, Steve Stratton, Janet Dean, Gary Strauss, Warren Throckmorton, Doug Rosenau, Mike Sytsma, Deb Taylor, Barrett McRay, Peter Ould, Christopher Yuan, and Mike Lastoria. Those who have been in youth ministry and have helped me translate our research into practical tools include Julie Rodgers, Liam Coventry, and Marc Santum.

Many months ago several "Side B"[1] gay Christians invited me into a discussion they were having about these issues. I am grateful to them for opening that door—Karen Keen, Wes Hill, and Ron Belgau, in particular. I hope this discussion continues for many years to come.

1

BECOMING A BETTER TRAIL GUIDE

PICTURE IN YOUR MIND TEENAGERS HIKING OR CLIMBING in a really difficult-to-navigate area. There are no obvious trail markers for them to spot. They are having a difficult time getting sure footing. They need help. That's where you come in. Your role is critical as a trail guide, and there are several things I want to bring to your attention to help you become a better guide for today's youth.

Teenagers who experience same-sex attraction or who are sorting out sexual-identity questions are navigating difficult terrain. You will be a better trail guide when you understand what they are dealing with and better grasp the unique developmental issues they are facing. You will bring more to your ministry when you learn how to establish an atmosphere of grace. You will be more effective when you learn to listen empathically.

The place to begin is with *compassion*.

Several years ago my wife and I attended a meet-and-greet luncheon for adoptive parents in one of the suburbs of Chicago. While I was parking the car, my wife went in to find us a spot at one of the tables. She sat down with a group of women and didn't give that fact much thought. When I joined her and the other guests, we realized that I was the only guy at the table. Then it dawned on us that the women at our table were all same-sex couples, and we were the only heterosexual couple at the table. It was a little awkward at first; we felt we had crashed the party, or at least I had. However, as prospective adoptive parents, we sat with the women at our table and the many other couples in the room who shared a similar interest in learning more about the process.

After the luncheon was over, we went out to our car only to find that it wouldn't start. The engine wouldn't turn over. I began to suspect it was the car battery, so after assessing both the situation and reflecting on my overall competence with automotive repair, I proceeded to give the universal sign for "help" by leaving the hood of the car up.

The next several minutes were interesting. I looked under the hood occasionally—just because it was something I could do to retain the impression that I knew something about cars. I moved some things around. A steady stream of luncheon attendees walked by on their way to their cars. For several minutes nobody stopped. Then a guy walked by with his wife, and I asked him for a hand giving the battery a jump. He glanced away from me and mumbled, "Oh, sorry, I have to get to a meeting at church." Great—now what?

Then, unexpectedly, one of the lesbian couples from our table walked up to us. One of the women offered to take a look at the car. She quickly confirmed that the problem was the battery. "I agree; I think you just need a jump," she said. "Let me get our car; we'll pull up right here and take care of it."

I couldn't help but think of the story Jesus told of the Good Samaritan. It is recorded in Luke 10:25-37 (*The Message*):

25 Just then a religion scholar stood up with a question to test Jesus. "Teacher, what do I need to do to get eternal life?"

26 He answered, "What's written in God's Law? How do you interpret it?"

27 He said, "That you love the Lord your God with all your passion and prayer and muscle and intelligence—and that you love your neighbor as well as you do yourself."

28 "Good answer!" said Jesus. "Do it and you'll live."

29 Looking for a loophole, he asked, "And just how would you define 'neighbor'?"

30-32 Jesus answered by telling a story. "There was once a man traveling from Jerusalem to Jericho. On the way he was attacked by robbers. They took his clothes, beat him up, and went off leaving him half-dead. Luckily, a priest was on his way down the same road, but when he saw him he angled across to the other side. Then a Levite religious man showed up; he also avoided the injured man.

33-35 "A Samaritan traveling the road came on him. When he saw the man's condition, his heart went out to him. He gave him first aid, disinfecting and bandaging his wounds. Then he lifted him onto his donkey, led him to an inn, and made him comfortable. In the morning he took out two silver coins and gave them to the innkeeper, saying, 'Take good care of him. If it costs any more, put it on my bill—I'll pay you on my way back.'

36 "What do you think? Which of the three became a neighbor to the man attacked by robbers?"

37 "The one who treated him kindly," the religion scholar responded.

Jesus said, "Go and do the same."

Jesus knew the heart of the religious scholar. This was a guy who was trying to justify himself. Jesus pushed him in an area that would be really difficult for an observant Jew of that day. He made the neighbor in the story a Samaritan. It is important to understand that observant Jews did not associate with Samaritans. Indeed, the Samaritans were considered unclean. Who was his neighbor? Who showed compassion? The Samaritan.

We all have people in our lives like the Samaritan was to the religious scholar. My pastor recently put it this way: God puts in our lives people each of us has a hard time picturing God loving. We have a hard time seeing them in all of their complexity because of positions the church holds. For many in the church today, gay, lesbian, and bisexual people are the "other"—those who are difficult to see with compassion.

What does this mean? In my work in this area for more than 15 years, I have adopted as a professional brand the idea of "convicted civility." This is a phrase that comes from Richard Mouw via Martin Marty. The idea originally was this: We have too many Christians out there who are strong on convictions but embarrass the name of Christ in how they relate to the world around them. At the same time, we have too many Christians who are remarkably civil, but you would have no idea what convictions they hold. We need both convictions and civility.

I think about this when I hear the word *compassion*. It reminds me of the civility part of convicted civility. But compassion is more than that. It refers to empathizing with the suffering of others.

Compassion is more than just being respectful with others with whom you disagree. But it's not any less than that.

Compassion is more than just refraining from saying, "That's so gay!" and "Stop acting gay!" but it's not any less than that.

Compassion is more than not passing along the latest gay joke, but it's not any less than that.

In *The Way of the Heart*, Henri Nouwen offers the following reflection on compassion:

> Let us not underestimate how hard it is to be compassionate.
> Compassion is hard because it requires the inner disposition
> to go with others to the place where they are weak, vulnerable,

lonely, and broken. But this is not our spontaneous response to suffering. What we desire most is to do away with suffering by fleeing from it or finding a quick cure for it. As busy, active, relevant ministers, we want to earn our bread by making a real contribution. This means first and foremost doing something to show that our presence makes a difference. And so we ignore our greatest gift, which is our ability to enter into solidarity with those who suffer.

Practically speaking, compassion involves truly seeing and listening to another person. It says, "Tell me more about what's happening in your life . . ." It involves trying to see her circumstances through her eyes (empathy). Compassion seeks to understand. It unpacks a person's story and allows a person's background and experiences to "thicken the plot" in that person's life.

Compassion also leads by example. It invites another to be transparent by being appropriately transparent first; in other words, it models transparency rather than demanding it from another and then being witness to that person's vulnerabilities.

Compassion is difficult for some people to muster, particularly in this area. Why is that? There are a number of reasons, but one of the most obvious is the culture war. By this I mean the ways in which people are reduced to political causes. If you start with the assumption that everyone in the gay community is an activist who wants to change the fundamental meaning of marriage, for example, then you are less likely to see the range of experiences among people who experience same-sex attraction, and your ministry will reflect that.

In the opening story of this chapter, I shared my experience meeting a lesbian couple who demonstrated compassion to me when our car would not start. Before anyone runs with the analogy between ethnicity and sexual identity, I am not saying that just as Jews of that day thought of Samaritans, Christians today think of gay persons. However, we have a cultural context today in which we have local communities of faith in which the climate is such that young people who are navigating this terrain cannot find any compassion. In fact, we may inadvertently push people toward the mainstream gay community precisely because we share the same tendency to reduce complexity to culture war. We appear to prefer politics to pastoral care.

CONVICTED CIVILITY

The phrase "convicted civility" refers to a balance between holding convictions as a Christian and communicating those convictions with civility.[2] It is a phrase that captures how I want to relate to others when discussing the topic of sexual identity. A few years ago I was presenting data from a seven-year longitudinal study that considered whether sexual orientation could change through involvement in a Christian ministry. This is not a question that is of interest to the mainstream field of psychology; and it is a question that is offensive to ask within the mainstream of the gay community. But for some conventionally religious people, such as conservative Christians, it is a relevant question. So I was co-principal investigator of a study that examined the question of change and also of harm. It was published in book form in 2007 and as a peer-reviewed journal article in 2011 (*Journal of Sex & Marital Therapy*).

When I was asked to present the findings at a colloquium at Regent several years ago, a local person who identified himself as an activist put out a call for others in the LGBT+ community to join him in staring down this "son of a [gun]" in protest of the study. The stage was being set for a rather heated encounter.

What does someone who is committed to "convicted civility" do in these moments?

I called him.

We spoke by phone a couple of days before the event, and I invited him to be my guest. (He was coming anyway, so extending an invitation did not seem too risky.) We shook hands and met before the presentation, and I met several of the other protesters. They filled the first couple of rows and indeed did stare at us as my co-presenter and I went through the data and implications for those in attendance.

We spoke again immediately after the presentation and actually several times after that. I've also met with others who came that day. Those exchanges led to an invitation to speak in Norfolk to a gathering of LGBT individuals on the topic. In the intervening weeks, I remember having coffee with one of the other protesters. He said, "You are nothing like what I expected. From what I had heard about you, I expected to see horns growing out of your head, and I thought you might have steam coming out of your nostrils."

This exchange, and many others like it, is the fruit of convicted civility. If we agreed on everything, we would have nothing to talk about. We would likely try to find another common enemy. But in disagreeing on some topics, we can still communicate about the nature of that disagreement. That is only achieved by treating one another with respect, by being civil in our exchanges.

I am not particularly invested in any one outcome in studying whether sexual orientation can change through Christian ministries. However, I am committed to identifying and researching topics of importance to the Christian community. We need psychologists who will ask the questions that are of concern to the Body of Christ. We cannot expect the broader, secular field of psychology to ask those same questions or have those same interests. Further, we need to ask those questions using the methods and procedures used by our peers in the mainstream of psychology. We have to allow good research to help us translate Christian considerations into meaningful points of dialogue with those in the mainstream of psychology and also the broader culture.

My point is this: *How* we discuss Christian considerations will be just as important as having those distinctively Christian questions and convictions. "Convicted civility" is one brand that might help us do just that.

KEY TERMS

Let's begin our journey into the world of sexual identity by clarifying some key terms. It's generally not all that helpful to refer to "the gay community" when you speak because there is actually great diversity within the gay community. So in this book I tend to use the phrase "mainstream gay community" to indicate what the majority of the members of the gay community tend to prefer. This reminds us that there are those within the gay community who disagree with one another. Take the topic of gay marriage, for instance. Not everyone in the gay community wants it, not everyone supports it, but I would say that the mainstream gay community is supportive of gay marriage. They support it, in large part, because of what it symbolizes (equality, dignity). In any case, by saying the "mainstream gay community" I am reminded that there are those who are part of the gay community who disagree with the mainstream of the gay community.

I frequently refer to "people who experience same-sex attractions," but I find that the phrase "people who experience same-sex attractions" is a little wordy and is cumbersome when used frequently. So I need language that will fit in a carry-on. I don't need long phrases when everyone knows what is being said—that needs to be checked luggage. So I'll often use the phrase "sexual minorities" as shorthand. In doing this, I know that there are readers who will not be receptive to that phrase.

The main concern I hear from those who are concerned with the phrase "sexual minority" is a fear that it plays into the political interests of the gay community—a community that wants to advance a particular vision of homosexuality as something akin to the civil rights movement. The rights debate has relevance to the legal issues surrounding gay marriage and gay adoption. I understand that referring to sexual minorities might carry some connotation that I support these legal arguments, but I assure you that my primary concern is clinical and pastoral. I am concerned with helping the Christian community find better and more helpful ways to respond to young people who are sorting out sexual-identity questions in light of their same-sex sexuality. When we depict the gay community solely in terms of specific political agendas, we tend to overstate what is intended.

My use of the phrase "sexual minorities" is really about numbers—the idea that it is not that common to experience same-sex attraction. To say it simply: There is a group of folks who experience their sexual identity *differently* than those in the majority, those who identify as heterosexual. Those whose sexual identity is same-sex are numerically in the minority, and so the phrase "sexual minority" can remind all of us of this fact.

Again, I realize that much of this language has been used to advance particular political agendas. So you may have to do a cognitive exercise occasionally to remind yourself that I am *not* talking about that here. I am not equating sexual minorities with racial minorities, nor am I suggesting that this is a civil rights concern. That is a different subject entirely, one that I am not addressing in this book. My concern here is with youth ministry: helping those who work with youth to be compassionate and speak relevantly to young people of this generation.

If you are involved in youth ministry today you will likely face similar questions about the language you use. What words should you use to talk about these issues? Should you reference homosexuality? Do you use the terms gay and lesbian? Do you talk about "sexual identity"? Or use the phrase "sexual minorities"?

I'll leave these questions for you to decide, but throughout this book I will try to define my terms so that the language I use helps you think about the issue with greater insight and understanding. My hope is that your work on your own ministry will reflect the complexity inherent in this topic—so that you can better minister to all of your youth, including those who are sexual minorities.

Again, let me define what I am saying: Sexual minorities are the students in your youth ministry who experience either their sexual identity or their gender identity *in ways that are different than those in the majority*. Sexual identity[3] refers to the act of "labeling" oneself based on one's sexual attractions or orientation. Common sexual-identity labels include *gay, straight, lesbian,* and *bisexual.* You may hear some kids refer to themselves as *questioning, curious,* or *queer.* Still others prefer not to adopt any label whatsoever. The difference between attractions and orientation is just a difference in the strength of those attractions and how persistent they are for a person. In other words, if a person has strong attractions to the same sex, and if those attractions persist and seem stable over time, they will likely think of themselves as having an orientation toward the same sex.

Gender identity is something different than sexual identity. Gender identity refers to the act of identifying oneself as male or female. People who experience their gender identity differently than the majority often report feeling distress or unease in response to their apparent gender as male or female. They may feel that they are really of the opposite sex, if not physically, then at least emotionally and psychologically. They, too, are sexual minorities. They experience their gender identity *in ways that are different than those in the majority*.

This book is primarily focused on sexual identity. So when I reference sexual minorities in this context, I am referring primarily to people who experience same-sex attraction. They are sorting out how to think about their sexual attractions and whether to adopt an identity that labels their attractions. For instance, they may decide, based on their feelings or attractions, to say "I am Gay" as a designation.

This leads me to one final clarification. I will capitalize the term "Gay" whenever I am referring to a sexual identity and more specifically, the Gay-identity script. I use the term "Gay" as an umbrella term for gay, lesbian, and bisexual *identities*. This will guard against conflating the noun and the adjective. In other words, we need to distinguish between the noun (Gay) that refers to a sexual identity and the adjective (gay) that refers to an orientation. I have not made this distinction in my previous writing; however, there are benefits to acknowledging that in our culture today "gay" is used by nearly everyone (and certainly most of the youth in your youth group) to refer to a homosexual orientation. To use it to refer to identity only will be confusing to them.

Another benefit to distinguishing between Gay as a sexual identity and "gay" as a sexual orientation is that it avoids stigmatizing the word "gay." Why does this matter? Because some Christians are finding it helpful to use gay as an adjective, as a way of describing and naming their experiences. While I know this is controversial, it has been an important way for them to name their reality in a way that saying "I am same-sex attracted" simply does not accomplish.[4]

Here is an illustration[5] that may be helpful in understanding the need for this distinction:

> In the world of hearing loss, you have those who are Deaf and those who are deaf. These two groups are well-distinguished and identified. Anyone who uses capital "D" Deaf knows she is referring to something more than small "d" deaf. People who are Deaf comprise a culture; they do not see themselves as having a disability. Instead they see themselves as a people group with their own language and culture. On the other hand those who are deaf do not see their hearing loss as an identity; instead, they see it as a disability or medical condition. This group is more likely to be "oral." That is, they often undergo intensive training to lip-read and use their voice to communicate instead of using sign language. Some might also seek a cochlear implant. When they say "I am deaf" they are *not* saying "I am Deaf." At times there is contention between the groups because of a conflict in how each group understands its experience of hearing loss. For example those who are Deaf see cochlear implants as threatening and an extreme offense. They don't believe anything needs to be "fixed." They celebrate their identity as Deaf.

As you read this book, I want to make it clear that I am not encouraging young people to adopt an identity label (Gay), particularly at this young age. While the use of *gay* as an adjective during adolescence may lead to *Gay* as identity for some youth, at the same time I recognize the importance of naming a person's experience. And I understand how some young people have found "gay" to be a word that does just that—without adopting the Gay identity.

If you are finding yourself confused and overwhelmed right now, let me encourage you to hang with me for a bit. Welcome to the world of youth ministry today. The simple truth that we cannot ignore is that we have become a culture steeped in sexual-identity labels. In light of these challenges, the question we want to address in this book is this: *What is your role in helping young people navigating this terrain?*

THE CULTURE WARS

Far too often discussions about sexual identity are reduced to the context of the "culture wars." When this occurs, complex matters about the causes of sexual orientation and whether it can be changed are reduced to sound bites. Nuance is truncated in the service of political causes—whether to advance an issue or defend against that advance.

Do you remember National Chick-fil-A Appreciation Day? Talk show host Mike Huckabee called for a special day to demonstrate appreciation for the restaurant chain Chick-fil-A. He did this after activists expressed outrage and called for a boycott of the chain because Dan Cathy, president of Chick-fil-A, had shared in an interview that he supported traditional marriage. If you were on Facebook at the time, your page probably blew up with people on both sides of this culture war sharing their thoughts and opinions. Essentially, who you are and what you believe about marriage and homosexuality was reduced to where you bought your chicken sandwich.

That's the problem with the culture wars. They take a complex issue and offer a simplistic solution.

FINDING COMMON GROUND

As the Chick-fil-A controversy was hitting the fan, I was in Aurora, Colorado. It was just one week after the tragic theater shooting, but I was not there to address the tragedy. Rather, I was at a meeting that had been scheduled several months in advance—a roundtable discussion with the National Institute of Corrections. We were working on a curriculum to train corrections staff in jails and prisons who work with sexual-minority inmates and juvenile offenders. Frankly, I was surprised that I had been invited, but the person coordinating the event wanted someone with expertise in both sexual identity and religion. Many correction facilities are located in rural areas that are religiously conservative, and they hire local people to work in these facilities. Since many of the staff come from a conservative religious background, they tend to view homosexual behavior as immoral. While they aren't necessarily acting inappropriately toward inmates who are sexual minorities, there was a tendency to turn a blind eye when gay, lesbian, bisexual, or transgender inmates were being bullied or worse.

I had been asked if there was a way to speak to religious people about safeguarding those who were incarcerated while still maintaining their personal and religious beliefs. We set aside differences in our understanding of sexuality and identified superordinate goals that we worked toward that would make corrections facilities safer environments for all inmates.

Jails and prisons might seem a little removed from your youth ministry, but there is an approach that works in both contexts: focus on common issues. When people try to reduce the complexity of homosexuality to a chicken sandwich, we would do well to transcend these culture wars *when we can* by identifying and acting on the pressing issues of front-line care. In youth ministry, this means that we intentionally seek to care for and minister to young people who are navigating sexual-identity questions and concerns—rather than alienating them or dismissing them.

If you are primarily interested in debates about the culture wars, this book is not for you. My hope is that this book will assist you in rising above the culture wars to provide meaningful ministry to the youth in your church. We cannot ignore the culture wars—they are ever present—but we can avoid getting pulled into the battles and skirmishes by speaking to the complexity of an issue with nuance, reflecting a pastoral heart, and change what pastoral care to sexual minorities looks like in the church today.

Unfortunately, and in large part due to the culture wars, much of pastoral care today has been reduced to an assumption that clear theological teaching about sexual morality is all we need. Some churches believe that if they are *clear* about sexual ethics—teaching what is right and wrong behavior—then they have discharged their ministry responsibilities. I am all for clear teaching on matters of sexual ethics. However, teaching alone is not a replacement for personal, relational ministry to people. Teaching can provide an important framework for a discussion, but it is not sufficient to address the struggles of individual young people today.

Again, let me be clear. The church does need to provide a Christian vision for sexuality. I myself have contributed to that discussion over the years, and those familiar with my writing know that I believe the church's historic teaching on sexual behavior is correct. God's revealed will for genital sexual expression is in a monogamous and lifelong union between a man and a woman.

That said, I agree with Andrew Marin[6] who has said that answering questions like these can end up closing the door to meaningful discussion about a topic with those who disagree. Some, like Andrew, have been more circumspect in answering direct questions, and I can respect their reasons for doing so. My own views on this matter have been published and are widely available, so I won't elaborate further on this matter. I raise it here to point out that simply teaching doctrine or preaching on a matter does not equate to actual ministry. Further engagement is required.

Again, this book is intended to be a resource to youth ministry staff who work with sexual-minority kids—teenagers who experience same-sex attraction or are dealing with sexual-identity questions. I hope that it will also help youth pastors who want their youth to be more informed about this topic so they can learn to practice compassion in an atmosphere of grace.

NAVIGATING DIFFICULT TERRAIN

Students today are navigating some difficult terrain. They find it difficult to get good footing. They need help. That's the image I want you to have for your students as they navigate the complex questions surrounding sexual identity. The current culture wars make it harder for them to see where to go. The terrain they travel is constantly changing. They are trying to make their way through adolescence and into young adulthood, and at the same time they are struggling with same-sex attractions. They are confused. They feel lost. They need guidance and direction.

As a youth worker or youth pastor, it is essential that you have this image clear in your mind. You need to enter the terrain that your students are traveling and appreciate how difficult it is for them. To fully understand the challenges they face, you will need to think about three key issues: (1) the conflict between sexual identity and religious identity; (2) the developmental process of identity formation; and (3) the competing perspectives from the mainstream of the gay community and from the local church.

In the chapters that follow, we'll look at each of these three issues in more detail.

So strap on your backpacks. It's time to start hiking!

CHECK YOUR COMPASS

1. Why do some people prefer the culture wars to ministry or pastoral care?

2. What are the advantages of keeping the discussions political or social/cultural rather than personal and pastoral? What are some of the unintended consequences when our focus is exclusively political?

3. What is gained and what is lost in relying on theological statements about sexual ethics to function as pastoral care?

4. In what practical ways would your ministry change if you adopted "convicted civility" as your ministry brand?

2

CHECK CONDITIONS: THE STORM CLOUD

WHEN I WAS A STUDENT IN GRADUATE SCHOOL, I enjoyed hiking and biking with a close friend and one of our professors, who was a mentor and is now also a good friend. The three of us would later write a book together—and if there is any way to test a friendship, it is through a collaborative writing project!

One of our trips was to Door County in Wisconsin to camp and kayak. The weeks building up to that trip were exciting. We anticipated several days of hiking on gorgeous trails and then kayaking around the islands that dotted the shoreline. But on the day of our departure, it rained. Not just a light sprinkle—a full-blown deluge. And it rained off and on the entire day. While we still enjoyed being together, we ended up cutting our weekend short. We discovered that difficult terrain is even more difficult when you hike it in bad weather. Add a storm to any hiking trip and you can bet you will be in for an adventure you hadn't planned.

In a similar sense, there is a storm cloud that hangs over any attempt to talk about ministry to sexual-minority youth—those who are asking questions about homosexuality and their sexual identity. This "storm cloud" is the conflict that often exists between the questions about *sexual* identity teens are asking and the questions they are asking about their *religious* identity. Adolescents who experience same-sex attraction aren't growing up in a vacuum. They have likely heard messages from parents, pastors, their peers, and the media that inform their thinking about homosexuality and their own faith identity. Those messages are often in conflict.

What kinds of questions do teens have about their sexual identity? Here are a few of the most common:

"Why do I feel attractions toward others of the same sex?"
"How did I develop a homosexual orientation?"
"How do I make sense of my same-sex sexuality?"
"What do my attractions mean?" and
"Who am I in light of what I am feeling?"

Remember these are *normal* questions for a person experiencing same-sex attraction to ask. They are difficult for anyone to answer, but especially for teenagers. And they aren't answered in isolation. Teens answer these questions in relationship to others: their peer groups, their local churches, their youth ministers, their parents, and others who have influence in their lives.

Most of the messages we hear about homosexuality today are "caught" not "taught." Young people "catch" messages about homosexuality, the gay community, and their sexual identity from the people they hang around in school, at church, and at home. While there has been an increase in the number of educational messages about gay and lesbian issues students hear in public schools, the reality is that very few people "teach" a message about homosexuality. Most of the time the messages conveyed are *indirect*.

What are these indirect messages that youth hear? Well, some of it depends on who they are spending time with. But some of the messages teens hear today include:

"Some people are straight; some are gay. I'm cool with that."
"Gays are going to hell. Period."
"People can do what they want. It doesn't bother me."
"I know gay people. They are just like the rest of us."
"If I'm gay, I am condemned. I'm an abomination in the eyes of my church."

Sometimes, these messages are stated directly. Sometimes they are implied. But either way, they are being communicated. And they aren't offering one message. Rather there are conflicting messages here. Some are affirming, some are condemning, some are in between. Hearing these mixed messages from different groups raises questions—about their own sexual identity and how that relates to their religious identity.

The questions teens ask about their sexual identity are further complicated when they are asked in the context of their religious faith. Now they are asking questions like:

"How do I reconcile my same-sex sexuality in light of my Christian faith?"
"Where is God in all of this?"
"Why doesn't God heal me?" and
"I believe God loves everyone, but why don't I feel loved by God right now?"

Some of these are questions about suffering: Why does God allow me to suffer with these feelings? Why can't I be healed? Where is God in what I am going through? Why do I feel I am on my own? Other questions might be about a person's emotional experience of God: Why do I feel distant from God? Why does it seem God is distant from me? I believe (in principle) in God's love, grace, and forgiveness, but why do I not *feel* God's love and grace? Why do I not *feel* forgiven?

Most of us aren't dealing with these tough questions about our own sexual identity and our faith in God. As a youth sponsor or pastor you may have had to reconcile your sexual attraction to a person of the opposite sex with the Christian sexual ethic. You may have wrestled with temptation and had to learn to wait to act on your attractions (fully) until marriage. Certainly, this is a difficult challenge for teens and young adults—especially for those who remain single throughout their lives.

But several additional challenges arise for those who are experiencing same-sex attractions. Sexual minorities never hear the message that they should wait until they marry. In fact, they hear nothing that resembles their own experience besides negative condemnations of "homosexuality" or "the gay community." They have no paradigm for understanding their experience—no models or examples for how to deal with their struggle.

Silence is not the answer. Silence creates a vacuum in ministry that is quickly filled by social networks, the media, and the entertainment industry. Silence says, "I have no idea how to be present in your pain and vulnerability. I don't know how to come alongside you."

I was involved in conducting a study that looked at the conflict that young people struggle with between their sexual identity and their religious identity, and one young person—who experienced same-sex attraction but did not identify herself as gay—shared the following with us:

> . . . I didn't label my homosexual feelings . . .'cause I grew up in the church and they said that homosexuals were the worst people on earth. When I did recognize my homosexual feelings, I went to a church that was very negative. I told a member of my leadership who told me to never tell anyone. It really

helped to solidify my identity. These people don't care about me. They said gays hated God.[7]

Figure 1. *The Storm Cloud: Sexual and Religious Identity Conflict*

Let's unpack what this young woman said. First, she recalled her church teaching that homosexuals were "the worst people on earth." This isn't the same as a church teaching a traditional, Christian sexual ethic in which genital sexual intimacy is reserved for marriage between a man and a woman. That may or may not be what this church teaches. What this young woman heard taught was that homosexuals are bad people—the very worst kind of people.

Imagine, now, that you are this young teenage girl. Perhaps you are 12 or 13 years old. How might this teaching affect you if you were feeling attractions to someone of the same sex? Would you be more or less likely to be honest about how you were feeling? Would you be inclined to share your feelings with someone else? Or would you hide them and hope and pray that they go away? Might you begin to hate yourself? Or . . . begin to hate your church?

My point, again, is not to critique the traditional view of Christian sexual morality. Instead, I want us to consider how the Christian moral vision is *communicated*—how a church talks about sexuality (in general) and homosexuality (in particular). How do we refer to people who identify as gay or lesbian? Imagine what it is like to be a teenager in that setting—to experience same-sex attraction at puberty in your faith community? Is there an "us versus them" culture war mentality? Where do you find yourself identifying—as one of "them"? One of the "worst people on earth"?

This is the storm cloud hanging over the church today. Every time you speak about sexuality, every attempt you make to minister to a youth struggling with these questions, you need to consider the storm cloud and how it affects the terrain your students are hiking.

Let's continue unpacking this young woman's experience. She goes on to share that she went to someone in leadership at her church to share what she was experiencing. She tried to be honest about her conflicted feelings. The leadership of the church—perhaps her youth pastor—tells her to never mention this to anyone . . . ever.

LOCATING THE STORM

Though we may sometimes lump young adults and teens together, there are some differences I've noticed between them—things I've noticed in my own counseling. Young adults often come to me because of their *own* conflict with their same-sex attraction. Teens come because of their *parents'* conflict with their same-sex attraction.

Because of this difference, whenever I work with teens in counseling today, I first meet with them along with their parents to get to know them better and to get a sense of what they would like to get out of our counseling time. I find that the teen may or may not agree with how their parents see things. They may not be at all distressed or upset by their sexual identities. I find that I can learn quite a bit from meeting with both the teen and his or her parents. Not everyone is always on the same page. In fact, given the complexity involved, it is not uncommon for family members to be in different places.

Some of the teens I meet with who have sexual-identity questions aren't all that conflicted about their attraction to someone of the same sex. Surprisingly, I find that these teens are often willing to come to me for counseling because it also offers an avenue for their parents to talk about their own conflicted feelings. This is especially true for the older teens I've seen.

At the same time, I have also met with teens who tell me that they *are* concerned about their attractions. These concerns might be from within—the storm is inside of them, and they are wrestling with their own beliefs and values. Or the storm can be a concern that others not learn about their struggles—a fear of peer or church rejection. Some think of themselves in identity terms (Gay) because they once felt an attraction toward others of the same sex. Others identify this way because they don't fit into rigid gender stereotypes for what it means to be a young man or a young woman.

When you talk with teens and young adults, it's important to identify where the storm is located. Is it within the teenager sitting across from you? Or is it between her and others in her life? Some teens will speak about an internal conflict, and it might sound remarkably similar to what their parents are saying. It takes work to accurately hear their "voice"—to understand what they are thinking and feeling. In some cases, they are still developing that voice and trying to define how they think about the attractions they feel, as well as how those beliefs and experiences fit with their Christian faith.

What does this communicate to this young woman? If she did not feel shame before, she certainly does now. Telling her to hide her struggle will only drive her toward greater isolation and make her more vulnerable to other influences. The negative emotions she feels, the confusion, now turn to shame and she learns that her feelings indicate that she is deficient, defective. We will discuss shame in more detail later, but for now it is enough to understand that there are ways we can respond that contribute to shame, and that desires and behaviors become even more powerful when they are forced underground—when they are kept hidden and secret.

In this case, the response given by this girl's church leader inadvertently solidified her identity as Gay. Rather than opening up a helpful discussion—rather than exploring what her feelings are and what they might mean—this response contributed to the "us versus them" polarization she has likely sensed due to the larger culture war. Her experience of rejection helped foster a clearer sense of identity within her.

Her church leader had an opportunity to show compassion, to empathize with her circumstances. He had a chance to talk with this young person and minister to her where she was. Instead, the opposite occurred. It confirmed to her that it is not safe to be transparent about her feelings (which leads her to further isolation and shame) and that what she feels is who she is (a Gay person).

Is it any wonder that she eventually concludes that there is no love for her, no place for her, in the church?

At this point, it can be tempting to think: *Well, I've never done that!* You may have never responded to a sexual minority in your youth group in this way. That's good. However, you need to recognize that it's not just a matter of what you directly communicate. The very same message can be conveyed without saying a word. In fact, not talking about the topic sends its own message, and it may be a message you do not wish to convey. As I mentioned earlier, silence creates a vacuum that will be filled by messages from our broader culture. There are unintended consequences when we fail to engage this topic in a meaningful way.

CHECK YOUR COMPASS

1. How would you describe questions that arise out of same-sex attractions? These were referred to as sexual-identity questions—can you name one?

2. What are religious-identity questions, and how are they different from sexual-identity questions?

3. Why is the relationship between sexual-identity and religious-identity questions referred to as a "storm cloud"?

4. Why is it important to "locate the storm" as being either within the sexual minority, between the sexual minority and others, or both?

5. How would you describe the messages you have been sending (either explicitly or implicitly) about homosexuality, sexual identity, and the people who are navigating these concerns?

6. If you hope to radically alter how you engage your youth around this topic, you may want to invite others in leadership to read this book and understand the rationale for the steps you are taking. Remember, many Christians have been influenced more by the culture war than by compassionate care.

3

MARKERS ON THE TRAIL: A DEVELOPMENTAL PERSPECTIVE

TO THIS POINT, WE'VE TALKED ABOUT THE NEED TO understand the terrain and to be aware of the potential storm cloud that hangs over any discussion about sexual identity: the conflict between sexual identity and a person's religious identity.

In this chapter I want to help you better understand how people who identify as Gay end up adopting a Gay identity. It's something I find most people have not thought all that much about. In fact, by default we tend to equate *attraction* with *identity*. Because of this, what a person feels tends to be conveyed through self-defining sexual-identity labels.

That process of adopting a Gay identity is a developmental process, one that has been extensively studied. Our knowledge of this process is based primarily on interviews and surveys in which adults (who may or may not adopt a Gay identity) look back on their lives. They share with researchers information about the key milestone events that they indicate were significant in the formation of their identities.

Based on this research, what do we know about the developmental period of adolescence—the teen years that are most relevant to your ministry to youth? Adolescence is a time of transition and change. It extends from the end of childhood until the beginning of young adulthood. Since the time of the Industrial Revolution, we have seen in the West a gradual lengthening of the adolescent time period. This is due to a number of factors, including earlier physical maturation, prolonged education, and the delay of financial independence.

Adolescence is also a time of significant physical, cognitive, and social development. Teens are growing physically, with the most evident changes occurring at the onset of puberty. These are reflected in an increased sexual readiness and continued maturity toward adulthood.

There are also changes in cognitive development. This refers to how teens are growing in their capacity for logical thinking, deductive reasoning, and abstract reasoning. Teens are beginning to consider hypothetical situations and learning to walk through various steps in a decision-making process.

Social development, one of the key contributions of theorist Erik Erikson[8], is another type of development we need to be aware of. This is typically seen in adolescent identity development through the influence of peer relationships and the emergence of social and relational roles. It is affected by many factors, including the popular media, music, Facebook, blogs, Twitter, and parents.

Erikson identified one of the key social developmental tasks of adolescence as "identity role versus role confusion." Part of the growth process during the teen years involves experimenting with various identity roles. This leads to the formation of close relationships and teens testing out different roles in different relationships. One author has compared this process to trying on an outfit:

> Youths seek their true selves through peer groups, clubs, religion, political movements, and so on. These groups provide opportunities to try out new roles much in the way the youth tries on jackets in a store until he finds one that fits.[9]

In all of this, we are talking about the process of forming an *identity*. To put it simply, the formation of an identity necessarily involves trying out different social roles.

Because of this, adolescence is a time of asking questions: "Who am I?" "Where do I belong?" and "In what community do I belong?" Young people are trying on different roles and identities in various contexts to see what fits well with their emerging sense of self.[10]

As the "trying on jackets" analogy suggests, it's not uncommon for these same teens to explore identities at school that are different than how they are at home. You can add the youth group or the soccer team or the larger church community. Teens will try on different roles and identities with the idea that at some point there will be a seamless transition between places—that is, in the hope that *who they are will eventually be the same across multiple settings*. They are forming an identity, a stable sense of self.

Others have expanded on Erikson's original thoughts at this point. Most notably, James Marcia[11] has suggested that a key factor at this point is the relationship between crisis and commitment. Crisis refers to the reevaluation or reexamination of prior values or choices. This reevaluation ultimately leads a teen to a new commitment in terms of decisions, beliefs, and values. Marcia suggests that there are four statuses (not stages that everyone goes through, but different ways of experiencing this time of reexamination and commitment):

1. *Identity Diffusion.* There is no established identity and no push to establish an identity. The young person experiences no identity crisis and no commitment to an identity at this time.

2. *Identity Foreclosure.* There is a commitment to an identity, not through crisis but by the suggestions of others. Here we see a tendency to conform to the expectations of others in their community or to adopt an identity of someone close to them, such as a parent.

3. *Identity Moratorium.* The young person is actively exploring identity options following a crisis but has not made a commitment to any one identity at this time.

4. *Identity Achievement.* The identity crisis is resolved and the young person is committed to an identity that's stable across different communities he or she participates in; identity is reflected in his or her role and values.

Marcia was not writing this with sexual minorities in mind. His theory has far broader applications, of course. Some teens will go through a process of identity development early and experience little difficulty. Others do this much later in life. The key is understanding that this is a *normal developmental process.* Just take a look around at your youth group. All of your teens are going through this to some extent.

Yet even though this is a normal process, the developmental issues faced by adolescents are more complicated for those who experience same-sex attraction. The psychosocial task of trying on roles and eventually consolidating an identity is even more challenging. To return to our hiking analogy—this is where the terrain gets a bit more difficult to navigate. If the normal developmental process is a weekend hiking trip in the mountains, think of the developmental process of a person with same-sex attraction as something akin to the show *Man vs. Wild* in which Bear Grylls is dropped from a helicopter—

parachuting into a rather inhospitable region of the globe and surviving off the land.

Since the normal developmental task of sorting out the typical questions of identity is far more complicated for these teens, they need help.

Bear Grylls has his film crew; your youth have *you*.

To better understand what's happening, keep in mind that this stage of development is preceded and followed by other stages of development. Again, this is a process—one that begins around or shortly before they start in your youth group and likely extends beyond their time with you, through emerging adulthood and into young adulthood, perhaps even beyond that.

STAGES OF IDENTITY DEVELOPMENT

Figure 2. *Developmental Context*

There are several models of sexual-identity development, but there appears to be consensus around three broad stages: identity *dilemma*, identity *development*, and identity *synthesis*. The first stage, identity dilemma, refers to the dilemma that young people experience when they have same-sex attractions and find that their experiences are markedly different than those of their peers. This dilemma is particularly acute in the lives of conventionally religious individuals.[12] In her study of Gay and ex-gay Christian men, Michelle Wolkomir describes the dilemma:

> The men's identity dilemmas were not abrupt realizations. They did not experience a few episodes of homosexual desire and then worry about being bad Christians. Instead, their identity dilemmas formed over time as their homosexual desires persisted, forcing the men to recognize these desires as part of themselves.[13]

The second agreed-upon stage is that of identity development. There may be differences of opinion about what occurs in this formation process, but many people are able to identify milestone events in this stage. Milestone events may include experiences of attraction, behavior, disclosure, labeling, and relationships, among others. I will discuss milestone events in greater detail later.

The final stage is that of identity synthesis. This refers to the end point a person arrives at that signals the person has achieved a stable identity that reflects how she experiences herself, how she wants to be known by others, and is a congruent reflection of her beliefs and values.

When we look at the mainstream gay community, most of the models showing how sexual identity develops presume that a Gay identity is the ideal outcome. This is based on studies of Gay adults who are now looking back on their developmental process. In our own work we have also studied the experiences of Christians, some of whom developed (or adopted) a Gay identity, but also those of others who did not develop (or chose not to adopt) a Gay identity. Keep in mind, as well, that some Christians adopt the word gay as an adjective to name their experience rather than as a label of their core identity. The fact that they use this word may not tell you anything about their specific beliefs or behaviors.

Many of those interviewed indicated that the junior high and high school years were a time when they experienced one or more of these milestone events—those that ultimately led them to adopt a Gay identity. This is important for you, as a person who leads a ministry or works with youth, to understand. It means that your ministry approach can lay a foundation for a more constructive response from the Body of Christ. This means there is incredible opportunity to minister to youth during these years.

The following table indicates several of the milestone events that were important along the way for adults who now identify as Gay and for Christian sexual minorities, most of whom did not identify as Gay at the time of our survey. It is good for you to be familiar with these milestone events, since many of them take place during the years young people are involved in your youth group. In their review of studies of developmental milestones, Savin-Williams and Diamond[14] noted that age of first awareness of attraction to the same sex occurs around age 9, while the age of first same-sex activity (usually defined as when one or both people in an encounter or relationship experience orgasm) occurs at an average age of between 14-17. The first experience of labeling as gay, lesbian, or bisexual occurs on average at age 16-18 years old. And disclosure to others typically occurs after that—at an average age of between 17-18. Most of the participants (86-95%) across the various studies reviewed of Gay young adults engaged in same-sex behavior—it was a normative aspect of their identity formation.

Population	Awareness	SSB	Label	Disclosure	Relationship
Christian Sexual Minorities[15]	12-14	16-17	17-18	17-18	15-18
Gay Young Adults[16]	7-9[17]	14-17	16-18	17-18	n/a[18]

Note: Awareness = first awareness of feelings of same-sex attraction; SSB = same-sex behavior; Label = first labeling of oneself as gay, lesbian, or bisexual; Disclosure = first disclosure to another person; Relationship = first ongoing relationship with the same sex. In our most recent study, 26% of Christian sexual minorities engaged in SSB; 11% adopted a Gay identity; 18% reported an ongoing same-sex relationship.

Table 1. *Milestone Events in Sexual-Identity Development*

Awareness, behavior, labeling, disclosure, and relationship—these are considered important milestones, then, in sexual-identity development among sexual minorities. First, there is attraction to the same sex, then there is same-sex behavior leading to orgasm, then labeling of self (as Gay, for instance), and finally disclosure to others.

These milestones can be aligned with the process of sexual-identity development as indicated in the table below:

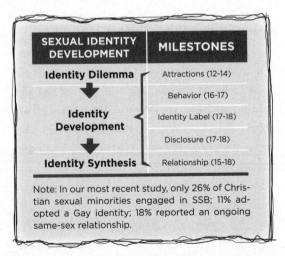

SEXUAL IDENTITY DEVELOPMENT	MILESTONES
Identity Dilemma	Attractions (12-14)
Identity Development	Behavior (16-17)
	Identity Label (17-18)
	Disclosure (17-18)
Identity Synthesis	Relationship (15-18)

Note: In our most recent study, only 26% of Christian sexual minorities engaged in SSB; 11% adopted a Gay identity; 18% reported an ongoing same-sex relationship.

Table 2. *Sexual-Identity Development & Milestones*

There are some general differences we should point out between adolescent men and women here. For example, females tend to report that their attractions, sexual contacts, and adoption of a Gay-identity label are more of an emotional experience born out of an existing relationship with another female:

> When reflecting on their early memories of same-sex attractions, female youths typically recalled crushes on friends; intense best friendships; and emotional infatuations with camp counselors, coaches, and teachers.[19]

In contrast, adolescent males tended to more often report "explicitly sexual memories—feeling aroused by the sight of another boy in the locker room or experiencing a furtive sexual encounter with a male friend or cousin."[20]

Another gender difference can be found in the timing of specific milestone events. In general, adolescent girls tend to adopt a Gay-identity label *before* engaging in same-sex sexual behavior, while adolescent boys tend to experience same-sex sexual behavior prior to adopting a Gay-identity label. Keep in mind, however, that these are more common trajectories rather than foregone conclusions.

We found similar patterns in our more recent study of Christians. Males tended to report engaging in same-sex behavior at a younger age than when they labeled themselves as Gay. In contrast, females tended to be in a same-sex relationship at a younger age than when they reported engaging in same-sex behavior or labeling themselves as Gay.

Again, it is important to stress that not all sexual minorities experience each of these milestone events. This appears to be particularly true when research focuses on Christian samples of sexual minorities. For example, in one study[21] we conducted of sexual minorities at Christian college campuses, we reported that while the average ages of those experiencing these milestone events were comparable, very few of the Christian sexual minorities actually reported specific developmental milestones that involved choices or behavior.

For example, engaging in sexual behavior is a choice, a decision a young person makes. Only about one-quarter (26%) of Christian sexual-minority students reported engaging in same-sex behavior. Similarly, adopting a Gay identity is a decision, yet only 11% of the Christian sexual minorities we surveyed labeled themselves as Gay. Finally, the decision to enter into an ongoing same-sex relationship is a decision, but only 18% of the Christian sexual minorities in our survey shared that they were in an ongoing same-sex relationship.

We saw similar results in a separate study published a couple of years earlier.[22] However, in our more recent study, we had more information on attitudes and values toward same-sex behavior. Christian sexual minorities who reported relatively less same-sex attraction and relatively more attraction to the opposite sex also reported more conservative/traditional Christian sexual values. Clearly this is an area in which much more research needs to be conducted, but there is a point worth making in presenting it to you: These milestone events may not be experienced by all Christian sexual minorities, and they can also be delayed as individuals are navigating the difficult terrain between their sexual identity (*Who am I in light of my same-sex sexuality?*) and their faith identity (*How do I make sense of my same-sex sexuality in light of my Christian faith?*).

With this in mind, I think it is valuable to explore in more detail the various developmental milestone events reported by Christians who experience same-sex attractions.

Initial Attractions and Confusion

In one study we conducted of young adults, we asked about some of their earliest milestone events. Most shared that when they were younger they felt different from their peers in childhood. This was usually around age 7 or so, which is likely shortly after they first experience greater exposure to a peer group in preschool and elementary school. They are no longer seen solely in the context of their family; they are now seen in a more public way, where they are compared to others in their peer group. For some Christian sexual minorities, this experience meant they were an outsider among their peers. Here is what one young man shared:

> Feeling like an outsider, like a freak. You don't belong to anywhere . . . you don't belong to guys. I had a lot of "girl" friends. Just felt like an outsider. And it was, when I was a child it wasn't really bad because I didn't really care. When I got in my teens it meant a lot to me as I grew up.[23]

Others said that they did not identify with others of the same gender: a young boy who does not identify with other boys; a young girl who does not identify with other girls. This was often seen in the choices kids made about play or other activities or interests. One young man shared this:

> I've never really been good at sports. I've been artistic and musical. That's always been a big difference that I've seen. And I view myself as not as strong as a lot of guys . . . physically. Felt maybe separate from a lot of boys.[24]

Some guys talked about not feeling athletic; others talked about not feeling attractive. Another young man shared about playing with dolls: "Playing with dolls with my cousin, but didn't realize this was against the norm. In first grade, I realized that other guys weren't doing that . . ."

Now we want to be careful in ministry not to see these experiences as indicative of same-sex attractions, as if young men who are creative, intuitive, and who show interest in the arts are Gay, or that young women are Gay if they are athletic or stellar in math and science and who are drawn to engineering. These are memories of young adults looking back at significant events in their lives, events that carry meaning for them today.

Many young people will not fit into rigid gender stereotypes for masculinity and femininity, so we must be careful not to make assumptions.

What is the takeaway for ministry? If a teen does not fit into gender stereotypes, that's okay. You can create an atmosphere that says, "That's okay. You are okay." We don't make assumptions that not fitting into rigid stereotypes means a person is anything other than not fitting into rigid stereotypes. That is perfectly fine. What we are not going to do is highlight those rigid gender stereotypes as though a person should feel inadequate for not "fitting in."

NO LABEL, THANK YOU VERY MUCH

When I first began conducting research on sexual identity more than 15 years ago, most people who participated in interviews or completed questionnaires selected a sexual-identity label. It might have been gay, straight, bi, or some other designation. However, over the years we have seen an interesting development. More and more sexual-minority youth are saying that they prefer not to label themselves at all.

Some people reject a label because it leads them to experience conflict with their Christian identity. For example, one young man we interviewed shared that he had *no label* for his sexual identity: "I would say no label. I can't really say I am straight because I am sexually attracted to men. Not homosexual or gay because I think those are identities and not fact. I refuse to identify as homosexual/gay because I find my identity in Christ and those are not Christ-like identities."[25]

This isn't just something we find in Christian samples. It's been observed in larger community samples and samples from students at public universities, many of whom are not identifying as Gay as such. In her book, *The End of Sexual Identity*, Jenell Williams Paris describes how both Gay identity and heterosexual identity are socially constructed and not "real" differences that exist across time and in all cultures. She envisions a time when we will not identify ourselves by our sexual preferences at all. This is difficult to envision given that we presently live in a culture steeped in sexual-identity labels.

Still, it's worth noting that there appears to be a trend among sexual minorities toward avoiding labels. What do you make of this trend? What do you see as the advantages to not adopting a sexual-identity label at all? What of the benefits some people report in naming their experience?

There are also noted differences between male and female experiences of same-sex attraction that appear to influence sexual-identity labels. Among male sexual minorities, about two-thirds will identify as Gay while about one-third will identify as bisexual. The reverse is the case among females, where about two-thirds of female sexual minorities will identify as bisexual and only one-third as lesbian.[26] These findings are consistent with the view that females may be more likely to experience greater sexual fluidity than males, a finding also demonstrated in a study[27] of sexual-minority women over more than a decade. In that study, it was common for the women to report attraction and sexual behavior with both men and women (even among those who identified as lesbian) and to change their sexual-identity label to reflect their current interests.

This highlights the diversity among those who experience same-sex sexuality. There appear to be important differences among sexual minorities who come from religious faith backgrounds and who see their faith as important in shaping decisions about their behavior and the identity labels they adopt. There also appear to be important differences among male and female experiences of same-sex sexuality.

This diversity needs to be taken into consideration as you think about youth ministry. Even a basic understanding of these milestone events will be helpful to you as you seek to become a better trail guide to youth with questions. In particular, this is helpful when you are talking with someone who is first experiencing same-sex attractions, as these experiences are inherently tied to meaning-making and a developing sense of purpose, which we will discuss next.

Meaning-Making

Perhaps the most critical area of difference we have seen in our research has to do with how young people make sense of their attraction to the same sex. We call this "meaning-making" or making "attributions." Attributions refer to the reasons people assign to their attractions. Do they attribute their attraction to an emerging identity? Is it a reflection of our shared, fallen condition? Or is it attributed to something else entirely? This is an area where those who are working with youth can have productive conversations, discussing possible reasons why a student has a same-sex attraction. I do not claim that there is one "right" attribution to make; rather I have been impressed by the role that attributions play in setting a person on a path. There are many possible paths or trajectories tied to the diverse ways in which people make meaning out of their experience.

Some time ago I was interviewed by a reporter about the way in which I do my counseling. I base it on a model I co-developed with Warren Throckmorton called Sexual-Identity Therapy. I was explaining how I do this therapy, and the reporter tried to paraphrase back to me to see if she understood:

"So, it's helping people change their thoughts?" I said, "Well, it's not just that a person has one kind of thought, and then they change it to another thought. That is not getting at the complexity of what happens. It's more like you help a person write the story of their life—so think of it more as a way of being, rather than a way of thinking, though thoughts are certainly important."

"You help people think about things differently?" she asked.

"No, that's not quite it," I said. I help people 'story their lives.' They write the story of who they are."

"So they change their minds, right? They think differently, is that it?" she asked. "Nope," I said. "We're not quite there yet."

The point I was trying to get across to this reporter is that how a person *thinks* about her attractions is not just a thought exercise. It is not like the decision to wear jeans rather than khakis, or like giving oneself a pep talk in preparation for a public speech.

Take Emma, for example. Emma has a narrative that shapes the way she thinks about her life. It tells her who she is, how she thinks about herself, how she wants to live, and so on. This story is an integrated and meaningful way in which she lives out her beliefs and unites them to her past and present experiences. Part of her narrative entails setting goals for how she will live in the future. It also involves establishing habits that support these goals and this identity. Having these habits and goals organizes her life and informs her choices. When Emma is able to live her narrative out in community with others who share her understanding of herself and support this story of her life, it gradually becomes woven into the fabric of her being.

Or consider another example: I can think of myself as "athletic," and I can label myself a "jock," but if I never take any practical steps to develop my athletic potential and foster the habits that would shape that identity—such as regular workouts, incorporating sustained cardiovascular workouts, building muscle mass, changes in eating habits, adequate sleep, as well as accountability in making and maintaining these changes, the thoughts and labels I adopt will be irrelevant to my lived experience. Furthermore, it will help in my strivings to have in my mind a mental picture of who I plan to become as an athlete. That end result is a reflection of the many ways in which I have "storied" that identity through the practical steps I have taken. Those steps cannot be merely reduced to my thought life or my behaviors. The end result of my identity is more than the sum of those steps.

Let's take a look at how this story has been written in the lives of various Christian sexual minorities who have shared their experiences with us. Most Christians who eventually adopted Gay as their identity[28] initially thought that their same-sex attractions signaled just that: a Gay identity. They believed that their attractions *necessarily* meant an identity, as did their sexual fantasies and the fact that their feelings of attraction did not change after they made attempts to change them. Some dated the opposite sex and used other strategies to increase their feelings toward the opposite sex, but these strategies did not work. As a result, they felt a sense of confirmation in their identity as a Gay person.

At the same time, when Christian sexual minorities chose not to adopt a Gay identity or engage in same-sex behavior, they tended to think about their attractions differently. Rather than seeing their attractions as signaling a Gay identity, they tended to assume their attractions were the result of a fallen world. Some pointed to strained relationships or other experiences as perhaps contributing to their same-sex sexuality, but relatively few thought of their attractions as being directly related to their identity.

As I stated earlier, we also need to acknowledge that there is now a younger generation of Christian sexual minorities who use the adjective "gay" to communicate to themselves and to others their same-sex sexuality. By this, they[29] are not intending to say anything particular about their behavior or their values. They may be celibate, or they may practice homosexual behavior. But by using the term "gay," they are simply trying to reduce confusion. They tend to reject labels such as "ex-gay," "post-gay," and even "same-sex attraction." They have found that these labels are not all that helpful to them in naming their reality, nor do they relate as well to the larger discussions occurring in the church and broader culture.

In the studies we have conducted, we have noticed that during the teen years it is not uncommon for those who respond—whether they eventually identify as Gay or choose not to—to think of their same-sex attractions as a longing for deeper friendship or an expression of a longing to be loved by others. One young woman we interviewed acknowledged her ongoing experience of same-sex attraction, but she was unwilling to form her identity around her attractions: "I still struggle with same-sex attraction, but I don't want to be labeled a lesbian . . . I've been trying to make a different identity for myself . . . it's a process . . ."[30]

Let's try to summarize some of this by taking a look at Table 3. This figure makes a distinction between common milestone events and the kinds of meaning-making questions that are relevant to a young person. Consider the time when most young people say they first experience an awareness of their same-sex sexuality and are attracted to another person of the same sex. This is a time when they are asking, *How do I make sense of what I feel? If I am female: What does it say about me that I find this person attractive, that I am drawn to this person and not to boys?* In other words, the meaning-making is tied to these initial sexual feelings.

As youth grow older and begin considering whether or not to engage in sexual behavior, that decision is also steeped in meaning and significance. The question of whether to engage in same-sex behavior can reflect worry or anxiety: *What would it mean if I liked being sexual with this person? Would I like it? Would I regret it? What would it say about me? What does not engaging in sexual behavior say about me?*

The question of identity often follows behavior for males but it may actually precede behavior for females.[31] In both cases, it is a question of how to name an experience: *How should I name my reality? Do I use "gay" as an adjective? "Gay" as identity? Do I move away from identity labels altogether?* In other words, what label do I adopt for myself?

The next major developmental milestone involves letting others know what you experience. This is disclosure (often referred to as "coming out"). The real question here is, *Who can I trust with what I am experiencing?*

SEXUAL IDENTITY DEVELOPMENT	MILESTONES	MEANING-MAKING
Identity Dilemma	Attractions (12-14)	How do I make sense of what I feel?
Identity Development	Behavior (16-17)	Should I delay or refrain from sexual behavior?
	Identity Label (17-18)	How do I name my reality?
	Disclosure (17-18)	Who can I trust with what I am going through?
Identity Synthesis	Relationship (15-18)	How can my needs for intimacy be met?

Note: In our most recent study, only 26% of Christian sexual minorities engaged in SSB; 11% adopted a Gay identity; 18% reported an ongoing same-sex relationship.

**Table 3. *Sexual-Identity Development,
Milestones & Meaning-Making***

Finally, the last major milestone discussed in most research is that of an ongoing same-sex relationship. Here the question seems to be: *How can my needs for intimacy be met?* The choice to commit to an ongoing relationship may grow out of a desire to connect with others, to form a sense of community and shared reality. A relationship can solidify a person's sense of identity. It can validate so much of what has been in doubt until this point.

As you navigate this terrain with students and youth, it is necessary to be aware of these key milestone events as well as the meaning-making questions your students are asking. Understanding these questions will help to foster empathy and compassion in you, and you'll have a better understanding of what they are experiencing—that there are multiple meanings associated with specific events. You can help young people by listening to them and exploring with them the meaning and significance they are attaching to an event.

This is where these milestones tie in to the narrative of a person's life. Let's take a young man named Trevor, for example. If Trevor makes meaning out of his initial same-sex attraction as Gay, subsequent behavior will likely confirm this meaning. This behavior, in turn, can lead Trevor to disclosure of Gay, naming this reality to himself and to others in a way that further fosters a sense that "*This is who I am as a person.*" There will be norms and expectations for behavior associated with this identity. If Trevor chooses to be involved in an ongoing same-sex relationship, this is a further consolidation of Trevor's storied identity.

Another young person, however, might experience same-sex attractions as a part of what it means to live in this world, but she may not necessarily choose Gay as her identity. Let's call this young woman Shawna. Shawna might describe her same-sex sexuality as "gay" (using the word as a helpful adjective), but during her teen years she refrains from same-sex behavior in keeping with the values that are part of her upbringing. Shawna's disclosure might be to let people know what she is experiencing, but she does this to foster greater transparency rather than to consolidate her identity. All the while, Shawna is active in her church youth group, she has been able to talk to her youth pastor about the challenges she has been facing, and she is pursuing a deeper relationship with Christ.

The point of these two examples is to suggest that milestone events do not necessarily have to cascade. Starting down the trail does not mean that everyone ends up at the same destination. There are choices along the way that lead some to take different paths: these are just the *common* markers along the trail, and most of them are **not** all that common among Christians who have shared their experiences with us. Indeed, quite often a person's religious identity and values play a significant role in informing the decisions they make.

What I hope you gain from this chapter is a more nuanced understanding of the "normal" developmental process that all adolescents go through (identity formation) and how that process has additional challenges when same-sex sexuality is considered. Generally speaking, I think it is wise to counsel young people to avoid prematurely assuming a particular identity (such as Gay). It is helpful to talk with them about the use of descriptors and labels and what they mean by them. The truth is that it may not be clear to them just how much attraction they feel to the same sex and whether this attraction will prove to be durable or will change with time. I believe it takes several years and greater emotional maturity for a person to distinguish between Gay as an identity and gay as an adjective. As a youth pastor or volunteer, you need to know that you don't have to be anxious every time a young person refers to himself or herself as "gay." This is an opportunity to engage them in further dialogue and I want you to have the resources in place to help you help them as they navigate this terrain.

While Christian sexual minorities report experiencing many of the same developmental milestones as their secular peers, they often do **not** engage in the later milestone events that reflect choices and values. Don't assume that these behaviors or identities are in place when you talk with a young person. Instead, try to foster the kind of relationship that is built on trust and openness, one in which they can share with you what they are thinking and feeling and talk about their experiences. Having knowledge of the full identity development process helps you to see young people with greater insight, understanding, and compassion as they share their experiences with you.

CHECK YOUR COMPASS

1. What are some practical ways in which a developmental perspective informs youth ministry to sexual minorities?

2. How would you describe the importance of attributions and meaning-making in sexual-identity development?

3. What are some ways in which you could help Christian sexual minorities explore meanings with which they might not be as familiar?

4. What are some specific ways your ministry to youth could be improved in light of the normal, developmental focus on identity that occurs during adolescence?

5. How would your ministry to sexual minorities be different if you spoke into meaning and purposes associated with important milestone events?

4

FINDING A PATH

LET'S REVIEW WHAT WE HAVE DISCUSSED SO FAR. WE have a storm cloud on the horizon. This storm cloud represents the conflict many young people experience between questions of sexual identity and religious identity. In the last chapter we added to this conflict some of the fundamental questions that are asked during adolescence: Who am I? To what community do I belong? These are normal developmental questions about identity and community that are complicated by same-sex attractions in a cultural context steeped in sexual-identity labels and fractured by the culture wars.

Add to all of this, now, the fact that our young people are often out there hiking *alone*. What do I mean? The truth is that most churches do not discuss the topic of homosexuality. When a church does talk about it, it is often done in a way that shuts down discussion. Teens aren't able to express what their attractions mean to them or ask questions about their identity. If anything, our failure to discuss the topic in meaningful and relevant ways is one of the things that drives young people toward greater isolation and the consolidation of a new sexual identity.

Figure 3. *The Competing Communities*

Teens today are also growing up as a generation that values the Sacred but is not particularly drawn to organized religion. Jeffrey Arnett, in his discussion of emerging adulthood (the time after the late teens and through the twenties), refers to the religion of emerging adults as "a congregation of one." The tendency of churches to be silent or singularly negative about homosexuality (in the context of the culture wars) may contribute to some of the skepticism toward religion and religious institutions that exists among emerging adults.[32]

In the West, we live in a cultural war zone in which people shout at one another about political interests that are also tied to deep questions about sexuality, sexual identity, and sexual behavior. This tends to truncate the complexity and nuance that is needed in any meaningful discussion of sexual identity today. Whether we are talking about activists from within the gay community or those from within the Christian community, youth today are hearing these competing voices, voices that offer little by way of practical assistance to them as they struggle with their questions.

READING FROM SCRIPTS

When teens watch movies, they understand that the actors and actresses don't just make up what they say—they say their lines and they do what's written in the script, a script that someone else has written for them. And like actors on a set, people act out "scripts" in real life as well. Many of the roles that we play in our lives follow a script. We may not read lines, but our experiences, the interactions we have with other people, and the things we learn from these interactions provide us with a script. That script can "define" who we are. It tells us what we ought to do, who we interact with, and so on.

Some will object and say, "I don't follow any scripts!" But let's consider a few examples.

Have you ever walked into an elevator full of people, pushed the button for your floor, and then turned around to face the door? Instead of facing the people behind you, you stare blankly at the door. You follow a cultural "script." We also have cultural scripts for greeting one another. The handshake . . . the high five . . . fist bumps. These are all greetings that we know are expected depending on the setting.

The Gay Identity Script: Listening to the Mainstream Gay Community

These are fairly simple and obvious examples. But in a similar way there are also scripts that make sense of our sexual identity. And there is a "script" for making sense of same-sex sexuality. I've called it a *gay-identity script*.[33] Again this is not an actual piece of paper you read to act out a role—it is a set of expectations that our culture passes along to people who experience same-sex attraction.

What is this gay-identity script? Being Gay can include understanding that:

- Same-sex attractions reflect *real differences* between people, not just behavior choices.
- These attractions accurately signal *who you are* as a person.
- Your attractions reside at the *core of your identity*, your sense of self.
- If you are Gay (as an identity), it makes sense to follow through and act on what you feel (your attractions)—because you are expressing and enjoying who you are.

There are also some assumptions about what *causes* a person to be Gay. They include:

- You are born Gay—it's just a matter of discovering this about yourself.
- If you have same-sex attractions but don't identify as Gay, then you're in denial or not yet ready to be honest with yourself about who you are.

My intention in presenting this script is not to pull it apart and show why it is wrong. Instead, I want to highlight a couple of things about it. First, this script has largely evolved as a way of providing dignity and worth to people who experience same-sex attraction. It is a script for people looking to story their own lives. In the past, when others storied the lives of those with same-sex attraction, the script was different. It said that they were an abomination (as people), they were mentally ill or perverse, and so on. Is it any wonder that a Gay-identity script has emerged?

Recognizing the importance of an identity script also helps us to understand why gay-straight alliances (GSAs) are such a draw for young people. Groups like this reflect a concerted effort to shore up an identity that has traditionally been vulnerable. Straight friends are also drawn to these groups, as they want to tangibly and practically demonstrate support for their friends.

Second, we need to understand that the Gay-identity script mirrors our broader culture's script about sexuality for teenagers today. This isn't just about homosexuality or same-sex attraction. Consider the script your straight teens are following. What are the messages they are hearing that form their sexual identity and influence their sexual behavior? Our culture associates our impulses with our "needs" and prescribes following our impulses to meet those needs. Our culture also highlights our individual autonomy, that we meet our needs independent of any outside sources of authority, including parents or religious values. The notion of "self-control" and "self-denial" fails to fit in with our broader cultural script for sexual identity. So the challenges aren't just in addressing same-sex attraction—they are related to broader issues in our culture.

I raise this simply to emphasize just how emotionally compelling a Gay script is to youth. Developmentally, young people are asking basic questions about their identity, as well as basic questions about their community:

Who am I, and to what community do I belong?

The Gay-identity script answers this question in a way that

feels right and natural to a young person. It fits with the sexual-identity scripts in our broader culture. The script makes sense to most people who ultimately adopt a Gay identity.

I think it's helpful to hear from Christian sexual minorities at this point, to understand what adopting a Gay identity really meant to them. One person spoke of the importance of community: "When I finally found a gay community, that helped a lot. I stopped wanting to die. Maybe someone will accept me."[34] Another person stated that he was on the verge of a psychological crisis, and that this pending crisis perpetuated the need to do something, which for him meant adopting a gay identity: "Feeling of absolutely losing my mind . . . it had to be reconciled . . . I needed to reconcile this for my psychological well-being."[35] Yet another woman shared about her experience. Although she ultimately chose not to adopt a Gay identity, she spoke to what it meant to give up the community she had with others at the time: "If I gave up the lifestyle, I gave up everything I knew . . . outside the [gay] community, I felt like a stranger in a strange land."[36]

There is much that could be said about these experiences, but they all illustrate that the Gay script meets people where they are. It addresses emotional needs. It provides a compelling storyline.

We will come back to this script in a later chapter. For the time being, I want you to recognize how common it is for individuals to adopt a script, how it meets specific emotional needs and assists them in answering the normal developmental questions that arise about identity and community.

The Local Church: A Community in Need of a Compelling Script

One of the reasons why youth in the church seek out a Gay-identity script is because they don't find a good identity script in their church community—not one that fully addresses their questions and struggles. Think about it this way: The local church is a competing community, and it is one in desperate need of a more *compelling* script.

Stop for a moment and consider your church and the youth that you spend time with. In a sentence or two, how would you describe the "script" that is given to a young person in your church who experiences same-sex attraction?

How emotionally compelling is that script?

How does it answer the fundamental questions raised at this stage of life about identity and community?

Our surveys of young people who experience same-sex attraction suggest that most churches do not talk about sex, let alone homosexuality. What kind of script develops when the church is silent? Others tell us that when the topic of homosexuality is discussed, it is presented in a singularly negative way that confuses people and behavior. Often, it is united to political concerns and agendas as part of the broader culture wars. Youth hear an "us versus them" discussion: "They (the gay community) are ruining this country!"

What does that script sound like to a 13-year-old boy who is beginning to feel a strong attraction to the same sex? It may end up confirming his sense of identity and community as he rejects the script his church provides and accepts the Gay-identity script instead. He tells himself: "I am Gay, and I do not belong here (in the church). I belong over there (in the mainstream gay community)."

What kind of script develops in the context of condemnation and rejection?

Shame as the Primary Script via the Local Church

When we have asked Christian sexual minorities about their experience in the church, many have shared openly about the lack of support they received. One young man offered this:

> I'd say it was really hard for me to tell other people with the same religious-spiritual beliefs . . . about my experiences with

same-sex attraction because I already knew what they believed about it . . . that it is immoral and I thought they'd think I had chosen to be attracted to same-sex attraction.[37]

Others have shared that having some clarity from their church about right and wrong behavior gave them a moral "compass"—it helped point them in the right direction in terms of delaying or stopping sexual activity.

While churches should provide teaching about the Christian sexual ethic, there is often a fine line between articulating these sexual ethics and imparting a message of shame. What, exactly, is shame and why is it something the church should avoid communicating?

Shame is an intensely painful affect resulting from an exposure of the self as flawed or inferior, and a concurrent deep belief that this deficiency will result in rejection, abandonment, or loss of esteem.[38]

When people experience guilt, they understand, "I should not have done that." Shame, on the other hand, says to them, "I should not *be* that." Guilt is about what we do that we should not do; shame is feeling bad about who we are. It is "the emotion resulting from self-condemnation along with a fear of condemnation from others."[39]

When people feel shame, they tend to withdraw from and avoid others. They may experience anger or blame others. Unfortunately, the responses of hiding, deflecting, and blaming do not really help alleviate the shame they feel—they perpetuate it. According to Veronica Johnson, there is a three-step formula[40] that describes how people develop shame:

Step 1: A person is raised in a culture in which various standards, rules, and goals are conveyed.

Step 2: That person does not live up to these standards/ rules/goals (perceived failure).

Step 3: The person then believes that not living up to

these standards is the result of personal deficiencies or shortcomings (negative global attribution).

We can apply this formula to the young person in the church who is experiencing same-sex attraction. He grows up in a faith community with specific standards, rules, and goals regarding sexuality. The standard communicated to him is that no one should *ever* experience same-sex attractions, that experiencing such attractions is sinful. If the church is not clear about how to understand these experiences, he will quickly surmise that it is wrong for him to experience these attractions, even if he did not make the choice, even if he does not want them. He may try to follow the advice given, praying and asking God to remove his attractions or change his feelings. If he does not experience success here, this will likely confirm in his mind (and to others) that he has failed. Because he cannot live up to the standards, rules, and goals of the Christian community, he experiences shame.

Let's think about how the milestone events we looked at in the last chapter might correspond with an emerging shame-based script (see Table 4). We begin with a young person in a church who experiences same-sex attractions. These experiences go against her church community norms and standards. They don't match what she has been told she "ought" to feel. Because of this she now feels like she is wrong (as a person) for having these attractions. And since behavior is a reflection of "who I am" (the Gay script), any behavior she participates in will be further confirmation to her that she *cannot* be a part of the church community—she does not meet the standards.

If this young woman chooses to adopt a Gay identity, she may experience some relief from the shame she has felt. Why? Because the Gay script represents an alternative storyline of value and worth for her. Adopting a Gay identity answers important questions about her identity (Who am I?) and her community (Of what community am I part?) in ways that significantly reduce the shame she felt in the Christian community. On the other hand, if she chooses, as a Christian, to remain in the church community and does not adopt a Gay identity, it will likely be difficult for her to disclose what she truly feels to others. Doing so will naturally go against the community standards and norms of the church community. Instead of sharing her experiences, she is likely to keep them hidden or secret.

Milestone events inform our understanding of how a shame script develops. But in addition to milestone events, we should also look at the messages and expectations we communicate about *changing*. What does it look like to change? One young woman we interviewed shared about her experience in a church that held out high expectations of "easy" change:

> The very radical Christian church I went to when I started changing built up a lot of emotions, led me to believe there was a simple change, therefore created a lot of resentment and bitterness toward the church.[41]

SEXUAL IDENTITY DEVELOPMENT	MILESTONES	SHAME
Identity Dilemma ⬇	Attractions (12-14)	I am different in ways that go against my community's standards.
Identity Development	Behavior (16-17)	My behavior reflects who I am.
	Identity Label (17-18)	Who I am (Gay) is bad.
	Disclosure (17-18)	I cannot risk letting others know me.
Identity Synthesis ⬇	Relationship (15-18)	I am not worthy of intimacy.

Note: In our most recent study, only 26% of Christian sexual minorities engaged in SSB; 11% adopted a Gay identity; 18% reported an ongoing same-sex relationship.

Table 4. *Sexual-Identity Development, Milestones & Shame*

Another person shared that not experiencing change was ultimately discouraging to him, and that he eventually adopted a Gay identity as a way of coming to terms with his same-sex attractions:

> Coming to terms with it, I finally got tired of being dishonest when I was 21 and tired of God not changing me.[42]

When church leaders communicate a message or an expectation of easy change, it can lead to resentment toward the church. We found that this message also leads to negative emotions that are turned inward as shame. Remember Step 3 in the formula for shame: a person believes that not living up to the standards is the result of personal deficiencies. He blames himself for not being the kind of person he should be.

Since the primary script that emerges from the local Christian church is that of shame, we need to ask if this script is truly the message we want to be communicating to those navigating questions about their sexual identity. Our research has shown that most youth who opt for the Gay-identity script find it more emotionally compelling than the identity script they are receiving from their local church.

A Gay identity provides meaning, purpose, and dignity to a person who would otherwise live in shame. That's why I'm always amazed when a young person questions the Gay script—there is so much at risk for him or her, so much potential for isolation and shame.

CHECK YOUR COMPASS

1. In what ways is the identity script as Gay compelling to a young person who experiences same-sex attraction?

2. In what ways could specific milestone events in sexual-identity development contribute to and intensify shame?

3. What is the difference between guilt and shame? How have you experienced these differences in your own life?

4. How does your approach to ministry change once you understand how the formula for shame affects those in your youth group who are attracted to the same sex?

5

SETTING A COURSE: WHERE TO BEGIN IN MINISTRY

HOPEFULLY, YOU SEE THE CHALLENGE FACING THE church today more clearly now. Young people are facing conflict between their sexual identity and their religious identity. They are asking questions, and these questions lead to conflicts within, as well as conflicts with their community. Those who work with youth need to understand the developmental issues young people face. There are normal developmental questions that youth ask, questions that are complicated by same-sex sexuality.

As this developmental process unfolds, we have seen that there are two communities that speak into the life of the young person. One the one hand, the mainstream gay community offers an emotionally compelling script that answers fundamental questions about identity and community. The church, on the other hand, has largely been silent or limited in its communication on the topic of sexual identity. If anything, the message of the church has led people to experience shame, rather than finding hope, meaning, and purpose.

First, successful ministry requires *compassion*.

Stop again and imagine yourself in the shoes of a teenager who is brought up in your church and who begins to experience same-sex attraction. Close your eyes if you need to. Let's say you see yourself as a 12-year-old. If you are a boy, you feel different than your friends when you hear how they talk about girls. If you are a girl, you feel different than your friends when you hear them talking about boys. You know something is different, and this difference is hard to pinpoint, but it seems to have to do with feelings you have toward the same sex—rather than the opposite sex. You begin to ask: What is different about me?

Most young people who experience same-sex attraction don't have a set identity—they are questioning, uncertain, looking for someone to talk with. This is where youth ministry is critical.

Some sexual-minority youth will ask themselves over and over, "What's wrong with me?" If she is a girl, she may wonder: "What if someone finds out that I get excited about other girls?" She sees how most of her friends are really excited about the opposite sex, but she finds herself attracted to members of the same sex. She might wonder: "Why do I feel this way?" She might feel frustrated, scared, confused, and ashamed. She likely does not understand why she has these attractions or desires. Even more, she has no idea what they mean . . . or what to do with them.

HOW DO I KNOW?

I was asked recently to consult with a youth minister. He had a girl in his youth group who seemed to be attracted to another girl in the group. They would hold hands during times of worship. They often sat by each other and hugged and snuggled.

A common question that many pastors and youth workers ask is this: "How do I know if a person is gay? Isn't it possible that she is just fond of other girlfriends and not really a lesbian? How do you know?"

This is a great question. Don't assume that you know anything about this girl's attractions or identity. She may not even be certain what her attractions mean to her. And what she believes might not be what another girl in the youth group thinks. Different teens may have similar behaviors, but they may not share the same assumptions.

It is also important to keep in mind that physical signs of affection are more common among girls than among boys at this age. Boys may tease one another, wrestle, and joke, but they rarely lie across one another, hold hands, or even hug each other (apart from "bringing it in" and giving "guy hugs"). So there are differences here among boys and girls this age, and it is unlikely to be helpful if you presume to label normal female affection as a Gay identity. In fact, doing this might inadvertently lead to further labeling rather than encouraging a constructive discussion.

Remember, a Gay identity is not a foregone conclusion. If it occurs at all, it is always a developmental process. The hand holding and snuggling might be part of that process, particularly if these behaviors are in response to attractions that the girl has given meaning. This is why it is dangerous to simply focus on behavior. More often than not, we don't know what the behavior or actions mean, and our true goal is not to simply change behavior, it is to speak to the heart, to explore meaning-making with the student.

Ideally, a youth minister or volunteer would initiate a discussion with the girl, avoiding a narrow focus on her behavior and instead trying to talk with her about how she is doing, how she is relating to others, about her interests, her likes and dislikes. It is hard to overestimate just how many conversations and shared experiences are necessary to earn the right to speak into someone's life about their sexuality and sexual identity. Doing so prematurely and exclusively focusing on this is likely to amplify any fears she might have. It may lead her to labeling or to believe that her attractions are the sum of who she is as a person. Again, the best place to start would be to foster a real relationship with her—a relationship out of which authentic youth ministry can occur.

Practical ministry needs a framework. The first four chapters have provided a framework for understanding the challenges the church faces today. Your role as a ministry leader is to walk with a young person as she navigates her feelings and attractions. To make this journey more manageable, I've broken down each step you'll need to take into a separate, short chapter. By reading each chapter and giving thoughtful consideration to the questions that arise, you will grow in your ability to walk with people navigating the terrain of same-sex attraction. You will begin to identify and empathize with the various paths a young person can take and better understand why one path might feel more compelling than the others.

I want to challenge you. Try to see all of this through the

eyes of someone who is attracted to the same sex. Know that they will face choices. There will be diverging paths. And you can help them make these choices, but you need to spend time reflecting upon the challenges they will face. You want them to make wise and informed decisions about how they live and how they will choose to identify themselves.

Keep in mind, too, that these are *their* choices. It is important that the teens you minister to feel like they are driving the decisions rather than being forced into something or manipulated. If they cannot come to their own conclusions and "own" their decisions, they will likely look back on their experience negatively.

As we move forward, we want to look at how to answer four common questions:

1. How did this come about?
2. Why did this come about?
3. What is my worth?
4. Is it just me?

HOW DID THIS COME ABOUT?

One of the most common questions I am asked is about the cause of homosexuality: *How did this come about?* If you will be talking with youth, you need to know how to answer this question as well. There are several theories about what causes a person to experience same-sex attraction or homosexuality. But the bottom line is that scientists *do not really know for certain* why one person experiences same-sex attraction and another does not.

The competing theories tend to fall into one of two camps: Nature and Nurture. Some say that same-sex attraction is due primarily to Nature—that biology through genetics or exposure to various prenatal hormones—contributes to same-sex attraction. There have been some studies of twins where it looked like identical twins were a lot more likely than fraternal twins to both be homosexual as adults. More recent research has suggested that the evidence for this theory is not nearly as strong as was first thought. Similarly, research on a marker on a chromosome was initially suggestive of a genetic marker for homosexuality, but follow-up research has not confirmed this, and in one case the researchers could not find the marker at all.

Others believe that the cause of homosexuality is Nurture. People on this side of the debate tend to think about influences from the environment, including early relationships and experiences. But similar problems come up when we look at evidence for Nurture or the environment shaping our sexual orientation. For example, a common belief among those who hold to Nurture is that sexual abuse in childhood is the cause of homosexuality. However, while a higher percentage of people who identify as Gay report a history of childhood sexual abuse, many do not, and most people who say that they have experienced sexual abuse in their childhood are heterosexual. It is more accurate to say that childhood sexual abuse complicates sexuality for those who have that in their background, but it does not in and of itself appear to directly cause homosexuality.[43]

Instead of seeing the cause as either Nature *or* Nurture, most experts today believe that there are elements of both that contribute to a person's experience of same-sex attraction. The specifics will vary from person to person.[44] Unfortunately, since much of this research is reviewed and discussed in a society steeped in the culture wars, it is very difficult to get a neutral, dispassionate perspective.

For what it is worth, I believe it is accurate to say to a questioning student, "Scientists do not know what causes homosexuality." This can be followed up with some other questions: "What would it mean to you to know?" and "How would knowing what caused you to experience same-sex attraction help you?" and "How would knowing with certainty change your life?"

COUNSELING TIPS

Keep in mind that the goal of your conversation about the cause of same-sex attraction is to convey to students that they did not do anything wrong in experiencing same-sex attraction. You want them to see that you understand that they did not choose to experience same-sex attractions. If appropriate, you could say: "Let me start by saying I appreciate you sharing with me this part of what you are feeling. I do not think you chose to experience same-sex attractions. I have not met anyone who chose to have same-sex feelings. Some people seem to 'find themselves' experiencing same-sex attractions." If it was appropriate to the context you could also say, "If you think it would be helpful to you, I'd like to hear more about when you first felt attractions to the same sex and what your attractions meant to you then and what they mean to you today."

You could then summarize what is going on in the debates about causes of homosexuality—that most experts today have concluded that we do not know about direct causes, and that both Nature and Nurture likely make contributions and the causes vary from person to person.

WHY DID THIS COME ABOUT?

Another question that often comes up has to do with meaning and purpose. For example, if there is a teenage boy in your youth group who finds himself experiencing same-sex attractions, this can be really confusing to him—and perhaps to you as well! In addition to the question of causes, there is the more existential question of meaning and purpose. We lived storied lives with implicit assumptions about who we are and our purpose and meaning. Eventually, all people ask "why questions" about purpose. "Why me? What is the purpose in what I am feeling?"

Since we really do not know what causes same-sex attraction, it may be more practically useful to be honest about what we know and do not know (about the causes of same-sex attraction) and then offer to listen to what students have to say about their sense of meaning and purpose. "What do you think?" "How do you think you came by these feelings?" "What do they mean to you?"

From a ministry standpoint, there is more to be gained in shifting the discussion from causes to meaning. As you talk about meaning, you have an opportunity to help students reflect on what they think and feel about having same-sex attractions, what these thoughts and feelings mean to them. Some teens will ask for help in telling others about their identity; others will want to know if there is anything they can do to have these feelings "go away."

As you talk, it is important to maintain a gracious, understanding posture. Youth need to know that they have done nothing wrong to have these feelings, and that it is good to have questions. You want them to know that they are not alone—that others are also navigating these questions, and that they do not have to make decisions in isolation. You want them to know that they have support from you as a leader in the church.

Try to keep in mind that the young people you are talking to will have to make decisions about how they are going to live and how they will identify themselves to others. They will need to wrestle with what all of this means to them as they try to live faithfully before God. So my approach is not to try "healing" or "fixing" them. I want to help them to find a path that is in keeping with God's will for their life. Does the path lead to healing? Perhaps, but at this point in time the focus should be on the journey, not the outcome. Focusing on the outcome at this point in the journey will place unnecessary pressure on students who are simply trying to get their footing on a rough path.

WHAT IS MY WORTH?

It is unlikely that students will directly ask you a question about their value and worth, but this is the question behind the questions you will be asked. All teens ask this question, and those who experience same-sex attractions often find it hard to talk to others about their experience. They find it hard to find people to talk to. And even if they do find someone to talk to, they find it hard to know what to say.

It is important that you communicate to sexual-minority youth that they have worth and value before God. You want them to see that it is God who ultimately gives their life worth and value. Your goal is to help them to develop a better understanding of themselves, their attractions, and the paths that are available to them. You also want them to understand God's revealed will regarding sexuality and sexual expression. Knowing that they have worth and value to God makes all of this less intimidating, confusing, and shameful for them.

IS IT JUST ME?

Finally, sexual minorities who are confused by their experiences of same-sex attraction often ask the question: *Is it just me?* They feel alone, different, and isolated. It is important to reassure them that there are many people who have feelings of same-sex attraction. Some may say that they have gradually developed their feelings, while others will tell you that it's just a particular person that they have strong feelings for. These feelings may simply be a longing to connect with another person, or they may be sexual in nature.

In one study 11% of teens reported that they were "unsure" about their sexual orientation and 1% reported having a homosexual (that is, attracted to the same sex) or bisexual (that is, attracted to both guys and girls) orientation.[45] Some teens adopt a Gay identity based on the attractions they have. Others choose *not* to adopt a Gay identity. Still others do not adopt an identity at all; instead they have an identity label placed on them by people who stereotyped them. When identity labels are assigned like this, they can stick and heavily influence the way students see their own identity.

For some youth, just talking about having feelings of same-sex attraction can lead to a lot of stress and anxiety. The idea of telling someone about these feelings can seem overwhelming, so they struggle alone with these feelings. But like any other burden, it is much easier if it can be shared with someone. Ask yourself: *Am I the kind of person whom others could come to if they were sorting out sexual-identity questions?* Is our youth group the kind of place where a person could be honest about that? When a young man experiences same-sex sexuality, he may decide not to tell someone because he assumes they will think he is to blame for what he feels. Our evangelical subculture attaches great shame with homosexuality, singling it out, and this makes it that much more difficult for someone to be transparent about his or her experiences of attraction.

Others may not believe it will help if they share with others. They believe that telling another person is not going to make the feelings go away, so why bother? We all need to know that we are not alone. And even if they feel this way, the truth is that it's a relief to find someone we can be real with, someone who lets us "fall apart" when we need to. Even if they act as if they don't need you or want to talk with you, the truth is that most young people who are navigating sexual-identity questions would love to have a youth minister who is knowledgeable and compassionate.

As we bring this chapter to a close, recall these steps on the journey thus far:

1. Navigate the feelings of confusion a student might have because they experience their sexuality in ways that are different than most others.
2. Talk about how this sexual-identity confusion has affected them and remind them of their worth and value before God.
3. While we don't know what caused their same-sex attractions, ask them about meaning and purpose as they begin to consider what they want to do about their sexual identity.

The things that we are writing about will not radically change in any young person's life over a short time. This is about a path. What is important is that those to whom you minister come to a place where they are clear about the choices they are making and how they set them on one or another path, and that they are at peace about the path they are choosing.

CHECK YOUR COMPASS

1. In the spirit of "How would I know?" if someone is gay, why is it important to focus on the relationship you have with the teen rather than on trying to interpret behavior?

2. What is an honest answer to the question, "How did I come to experience same-sex attraction?"

3. What are the benefits of discussing meaning and purpose rather than causes of same-sex sexuality?

4. What qualities do people possess that make teens believe they could talk to them about their sexual identity?

6

LEARNING
TO READ MAPS

THERE ARE HEATED DEBATES TODAY ABOUT WHETHER or not a person's sexual orientation can *change*. Some say it can. Others say it cannot, certainly not as a result of counseling or ministry. Some will say that this is just how people are "wired," while others may believe that sexual orientation is more fluid. Still others hold that if a person's orientation changes, it is probably not because of any counseling that has been done. On the other hand, there are many who believe that we will eventually find new ways to bring about change. The important thing to realize is that there are good people on both sides of this debate.

Along with this, however, there are also many assumptions being made. Counselors don't always agree about what they mean when they refer to sexual orientation. How can you talk about "changing" something that you can't even define? Moreover, does a focus on changing orientation get at the heart of the matter? As I have argued, focusing on "changing" orientation may simply raise expectations—expectations that may not be met when a person struggles and fails to change.

Instead of focusing on orientation or on changing a person's orientation, I have found it more helpful to talk about sexual identity. Recall that a sexual identity is how people choose to label themselves in light of the attractions they feel. In other words, sexual identity refers to how you identify yourself—as heterosexual, Gay or gay, lesbian, bisexual, questioning, and so on. This naming can be public (how you present yourself to others) or private (how you think of yourself when you are alone).

There are several components to a sexual identity. These include the following:

- Whether you are biologically male or female
- How masculine or feminine you feel
- The amount and kind of sexual attraction you feel (toward the same or opposite sex or both)
- How you intend to act, the kind of person you intend to become
- Your beliefs and values about sexual behavior
- Your behaviors (based on how you feel, what you intended)

While a focus on sexual orientation or changing a sexual orientation can be quite limiting, talking about a person's sexual identity can broaden the discussion and lead to fruitful dialogue.

Talking about sexual identity keeps the conversation in the realm of description, rather than jumping to fixed labels, and as you converse with youth you will likely find that a description is far more helpful than a label. What's the difference? Well, instead of saying "I am Gay" (as a label), a young person might say: "I'm a guy/girl who experiences same-sex attractions." By describing what they are feeling or experiencing, they have the opportunity to look at other aspects of their identity before labeling themselves based on their sexuality.

At this point, a person might object. "Since I experience same-sex attractions, doesn't that *make* me Gay?" Well, not necessarily. That's the point of talking about sexual identity. There are basically three ways to describe yourself in light of your same-sex attractions:

1. The first way is primarily *descriptive*. An individual might describe himself as "someone who experiences same-sex attractions."

2. The second way is with more of an *orientation*. An individual might describe himself or herself as "someone who is only attracted to guys/girls" (homosexual/lesbian orientation) or as someone who is "attracted to both guys and girls" (bisexual orientation). Some will find it helpful to use words like "gay" to convey this orientation.

3. The third way is by adopting an *identity*. An individual might describe himself as "someone whose identity is connected to my same-sex attractions" (a Gay identity).

At the most basic level, there are folks who experience same-sex attraction. Some may also identify as Gay while others choose not to adopt a gay identity. Still others use gay to refer to their orientation and to reflect their experience (Side B gay Christians[46]). Among those who adopt a Gay identity, some believe that being in a same-sex relationship is morally permissible (Side A Gay Christians).

Among those who do **not** adopt a Gay identity or who use gay as an adjective, some refer to themselves as ex-gay. Others prefer post-gay (to speak more to a trajectory rather than a change in orientation or attractions, per se). There are also others who adopt an identity "in Christ" rather than focus on their sexuality or same-sex attractions. Other possible identities include struggler or overcomer. Still others prefer no label whatsoever.

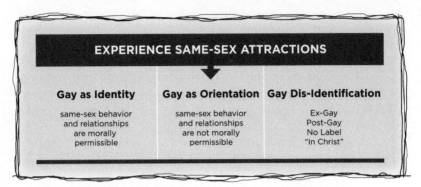

Figure 4. *The Many Ways to Be a Sexual Minority*

Again, my point in sharing all of this is to illustrate that there *are many ways to be a sexual minority*. Pastoral care and ministry varies considerably from person to person, based on these different ways of being a sexual minority.

HOW MANY SEXUAL-MINORITY TEENS ARE THERE?

This question is not easy to answer. Much depends on the language researchers use when they survey adolescents. Teens could be asked about same-sex behavior, as in the National Longitudinal Study of Adolescent Health study (Add Health). In this study, about 1% of both male and female teens (surveyed at ages 16 and 17) reported engaging in same-sex behavior, but again, much depends on what kind of sexual behavior we are talking about.[47] The percentages are likely higher for more common sexual behaviors, such as oral sex, petting, and mutual masturbation.[48]

Teens have also been asked about attraction toward the same sex. In this case, between 4-7% of teens acknowledged same-sex attraction. Teens have been asked about identity, and between 1-3% of older adolescents/emerging adults identified as gay, lesbian, or bisexual in the Add Health study.[49]

Interestingly, many people wonder how stable sexuality is among teens. In the Add Health study, heterosexual attractions and behavior accounted for the stability seen in that study. There was quite a bit of "migration" toward heterosexuality among adolescents who initially reported same-sex attraction or behavior over time, though some migration went in the other direction as well, toward non-heterosexuality.[50]

All of this should tell a youth pastor that there are many variables (and therefore possible pathways) that can influence an adolescent's sexual identity. Those variables include sexual behavior and experiences, sexual attractions and how to make sense of them, and sexual-identity labels and their meaning. There is a tendency within our church culture and broader society to think about people in rigid categories of Gay or straight. We believe that if an adolescent is not 100% heterosexual, then they are Gay. But the research doesn't support this. Instead when we look at behaviors/experiences, attractions, and identity, we see that there are many experiences that can raise questions in a teenager's mind, causing them to ask if they are 100% heterosexual. These experiences not only vary considerably, but they may be rather fluid and change over time. They do not necessarily equate with being Gay, and youth pastors would do well to avoid ministering out of these rigid categories, as they will likely contribute to confusion or premature and unnecessary identity labels.[51] Rather, pastoral ministry to teens can focus on navigating this terrain, creating a place for them to explore meaning and purpose, and anchoring their identity ultimately in the relationship they pursue with Christ.

THREE WAYS TO TALK ABOUT YOUR EXPERIENCE

Instead of talking about having a Gay identity, I find that it is more helpful for teens to talk about experiencing same-sex attractions. A teenage girl can simply describe what she *feels*— she has feelings for the same sex—rather than saying something about the kind of person she *is*. At the most basic and descriptive level, she can talk about having experiences of same-sex attraction, their intensity and how long they last, and what events or relationships make her feelings of attraction stronger.

A homosexual orientation is a bit different from simply describing experiences and feelings. It refers to sexual attractions to the same sex that have been around for some time. Referring to a homosexual orientation *can* be descriptive and helpful in sorting out feelings, but it can also be a further step toward making claims about one's identity. When people begin to label themselves in this way, they reinforce an identity label by behaving in ways that are consistent with that category. So, for example, if one of the guys in your youth group calls himself a skater/skateboarder, he probably wears clothing that is associated with skating. And because he has labeled himself as a skater, he is more likely to say things that you expect a skater would say. Along with this, it will become more clear to him as he labels himself this way just who is and who is not a skater, and he will start to set himself apart as an "in-group" member of the skate culture.

In the same way, identifying oneself by means of a sexual orientation label can lead people to see themselves a particular way, as a different kind of person (Gay). That said, using "a homosexual orientation" is not necessarily a move to a full-blown identity. We also use this phrase to describe how much and how often a person experiences same-sex attraction. Most people today will refer to this person as gay, and it can be helpful to keep in mind that the word gay is frequently used as an adjective to describe orientation or to name a person's reality in ways that "same-sex attraction" does not.

The word "gay" can be shorthand for the fact that stable, enduring attractions are there . . . *or* Gay can mean more than that. It can refer to an identity for that person. People who adopt the word "Gay" to convey identity will typically describe themselves *publicly* by saying, "I am Gay." But you may also find someone who is simply trying to tell you about his orientation: He is gay. Some see their attractions to other members of the same sex as one of the most important parts of who they are. Other aspects of their identity seem less important and may even be dismissed. Again, all of this gets at the deeper issue of identity. A person's identity determines the choices he or she makes in life. And the more central something is to his or her identity, the more it will influence the choices that are made. When an identity is centered on more than just sexuality or sexual attractions, it leaves a person greater room to make choices about his or her behaviors, thoughts, and feelings.

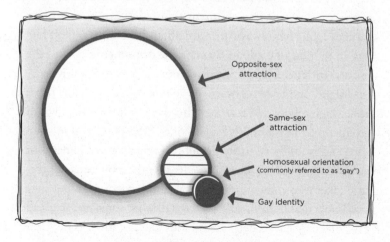

Figure 5. *A Three-Tiered Distinction*

For some of the students in your youth group, experiencing attraction to the same sex will be very distressing, especially if they have grown up in a household that has strong views about homosexuality or homosexual behavior. In trying to figure out how to deal with their feelings, some teens may become obsessive. They will try to avoid these attractions because they find that it's all they can think about. Consider it this way: If you were told, "Don't think about a blue bear!" you would most likely find yourself thinking about that blue bear! In a similar way, the harder a teen tries **not** to think about same-sex attractions, the more distressed he or she may feel.

With students who have questions, you'll want to let them know that these feelings can simply be descriptive—that they don't need to label them. Remind them that they are more than their experiences of same-sex attraction, as important as they may be to them. Talk about their other interests as well, their unique gifts, hobbies, and talents. The areas in which they hope to grow. Any other roles they have.

For example, you may have a girl in your youth group who is the youngest of five children (two older sisters, two older brothers). She has always dreamed about becoming a pilot. She has an interest in computers and is the drummer in a band she formed with her friends. She plays forward in a competitive soccer league. In her spare time, she volunteers as a peer mediator at her high school and is actively involved in her church's youth group as one of the youth leaders. She's been on several mission trips and would love to fly doctors and medical equipment for ministry purposes in the future. Her friends know her as a practical joker who comes up with crazy, spontaneous gags, but they also know that if they really need to talk with someone, she is all ears. She may have a deep love of kids and is known as the "fun older cousin" by the younger kids in her extended family. Someday, she might think that she'd like to have her own . . . and yet, in the midst of all this, she experiences same-sex attraction.

Talking about this one aspect of her life does not even begin to touch the depth of who she is, nor does it appreciate the complexity of her identity. In fact, it can seem quite limiting to *only* consider her same-sex attractions when talking about how she feels, let alone defining herself or forming her identity. After all, this is just one aspect of her experience.

From a ministry perspective, it is important to see the tension that exists between delaying identity and naming experience. I encourage young people to wait to adopt an identity label until they are older and more mature. The longer they delay, the more maturity they bring to the decisions they make about their sexual identity. At the same time, it is important that young people are able to name their experience. Keep in mind that same-sex *attractions* are reported more often among adolescents and emerging adults than same-sex *behavior*, and both same-sex attractions and behavior are reported more often than a Gay *identity*. I think it is important for a ministry leader to avoid prescribing how a person should respond. Instead, a person can help by discussing various strategies a young person can consider to navigate these issues.

Why the cautious approach? Since there are many unknowns in talking about these issues, labels can be prematurely adopted and a leader can end up setting a student on a course that makes other decisions less purposeful, lacking intentionality. A young person needs to name his experiences and needs to have those experiences validated. For some, simply being able to describe their same-sex attractions will be a way for them to name and validate what they have experienced. For others, "same-sex attractions" will not be sufficient. They may prefer to say, "I'm gay." Yet even here, I would caution a youth minister to avoid responding negatively. A strong reaction could drive a young person away or actually *confirm* a shift from gay as description to Gay as central identity script. Instead, this is a time for grace and empathy: "Thank you for sharing this part of you with me; I'd like to hear more about your experience . . ." is a better posture to take than "That's not right."

As helpful as this three-tiered distinction can be, I would also caution against using it to prescribe how a person should name his or her experiences. Allow the three-tiered distinction to be a ministry resource—one that is flexible, facilitating discussion in an atmosphere of grace. And remember to take the long view. How a student names their experience today may not be how they name their experience a year from now or two years from now. Remember, you are helping them to navigate terrain. The focus is not yet on arriving at a destination.

RETURNING TO SCRIPTS

In chapter 4, I introduced you to the idea that there are cultural expectations for behavior, what we commonly call "scripts." We talked about something called a "Gay-identity script" that represents the mainstream way of thinking about oneself in light of one's same-sex sexuality. At this point, I am not passing judgment on the script. I am just describing it as a reality.

I shared that the main parts of this Gay identity script include the following:

- Same-sex attractions reflect real differences between types of people (that is, Gay, straight, and bisexual persons).
- These attractions accurately reflect who you are as a person.
- Your attractions ought to reside at the core of your identity, your sense of self.
- If you are Gay (as identity), it makes sense to follow through and act out on what you feel (your attractions)— because you are expressing and enjoying who you are.

Following closely on the heels of this Gay-identity script are common claims about what causes a person to be Gay and about who you really are:

- You are born Gay—it's just a matter of discovering this about yourself; and
- If you have same-sex attractions but don't identify as Gay, then you're in denial or not yet ready to be honest with yourself and others about who you are.

When talking with youth, it is important to highlight the options available to them. Encourage them to see that it is possible to have same-sex attractions or a homosexual orientation (as gay) and not name this as identity (Gay). It is also possible for a person to describe himself as gay but not act on his attractions. In other words, there are many ways to *be* a sexual minority, and no one storyline should trump the others, no matter how common that story occurs in our culture.

Let's revisit this last point. Some students will choose to define their experiences of same-sex attraction in ways that are consistent with this dominant narrative simply because they haven't heard a different story. Yet there are problems with the dominant narrative. It may not accurately reflect a person's beliefs, values, or goals. For example, I met with a mother who talked about her 8-year-old daughter as a "bad seed," referring to her temperament and behavior. I found out that this girl was also grieving the loss of her father, who had recently left the family. The language of being a "bad seed" could have quickly become the dominant or controlling story about this 8-year-old child. If it had, it would have likely led to a very difficult future for her and her mother. What was needed was a counter-narrative—an alternative story.

A counter-narrative is a different story about a person. It challenges the assumptions behind the dominant narrative. With this 8-year-old girl, I helped her mother see other parts to her child beyond her temperament and behavior. I talked with her about how her daughter was grieving the loss of her father, that she was confused and sad. I also wanted the daughter to be able to work through this significant loss. Eventually, she could learn new behaviors (and could be rewarded for these new and better choices) and grow in ways that reflected greater respect, obedience, patience, and self-control. Right now, however, there were a lot of really awful feelings inside that were primarily the result of choices *other people* had made, choices that had hurt her. She was not a "bad seed" (the dominant narrative in her life). She was a "hurting child" (the counter-narrative I introduced).

DOMINANT NARRATIVES	COUNTER-NARRATIVE
Same-sex attractions reflect real differences between types of people (that is, Gay, straight, and bisexual persons).	Same-sex attractions or orientations are a reflection of a fallen world in which we live.
These attractions accurately reflect who you are as a person.	Same-sex attractions or orientation are an important part of your experience, but there are many important facets to who you are, and you have choices to make about what weight you give to these various facets.
Your attractions ought to reside at the core of your identity, your sense of self.	For some people, choosing a Gay identity limits other options or identities.
If you are Gay (as identity), it makes sense to follow through and act out on what you feel (your attractions)—because you are expressing and enjoying who you are.	Having same-sex attractions or orientation (as gay) doesn't mean that a person has to either identify with them or act on them. Many people with same-sex attractions aren't in a same-sex relationship or have not acted on them. I can take a broader view of my sexuality (than just my impulses) and learn more about myself.

Table 5. *Dominant Narrative and Counter-Narrative*

So what is the counter-narrative to the Gay-identity script? What is the alternative to the story we hear about in the media? The counter-narrative is more than just one story—it is many.

In fact, there are as many alternative stories as there are people who do **not** adopt Gay as their identity. There are Christians who experience same-sex attractions but who choose to read from a variety of other scripts, and the church benefits from hearing their stories.

One counter-narrative is to use the word "gay" as an adjective referring to a person's same-sex sexuality. Some Christians choose to describe themselves as gay as shorthand for the fact that they are attracted to others of the same sex. They may use the term, but it doesn't indicate the choices they have made about their sexual behavior (if they remain celibate, for instance).

Others make choices about their identity, choosing not to adopt Gay as an identity or to use gay as an adjective. They might use other words to express their sense of identity. I have mentioned several of these, phrases like post-gay, "in Christ," or overcomer. Others might prefer to think of themselves as a man or a woman (rather than reference their attractions). Others will identify more with their role as a daughter/son or wife/husband. Still others might decide to drop identity labels altogether as a way of reminding themselves and others that they are more than the sum of their attractions. In all of these cases, we need to realize that these are individuals who are making meaning out of their experiences in ways that run contrary to the existing Gay script.

What does this look like for teenagers who are experiencing same-sex attraction and asking questions? Here is a flowchart of the choices that exist:

	ATTRACTIONS ➡	IDENTITY ➡	BEHAVIOR
Is it a choice?	No.	Yes.	Yes.

Table 6. *Is it a Choice?*

If you understand what this chart means, you will be a few miles ahead of most of the people in the church today. Most commonly, people are confused about what qualifies as a *choice*. Many conservatives in the church continue to act as if young people choose to experience attraction to the same sex. Then they blame them for what they are feeling. But research has indicated that these attractions, for the most part, appear to arise and are **not** chosen. Still, that's not the end of the discussion. People do have choices to make about their behavior and identity.

Of course, you also find those on the flipside who believe same-sex attractions negate the additional questions of behavior and identity. Well . . . no, that's *precisely* where a person has choices to make. A youth minister can be part of a supportive community that helps young people make more informed, responsible choices about both their identity and behavior.

In one study of thousands of teenagers, the percentage of teens who experienced same-sex attraction was almost three times as much as those who identified as Gay. This means that while there are many more people who have same-sex attraction, only a small group of people later adopted a Gay identity. This indicates that most teenagers who experience same-sex attraction choose to follow an "alternate script." Since teenagers are known for wanting to be original, this makes a lot of sense! As a person who cares for and ministers to youth, my hope is that you will be able to provide them with options as you help them to sort out their sexual-identity questions.

CHECK YOUR COMPASS

1. As a youth minister, if you had to describe yourself (your identity) in a few sentences, what would you say? Comment on different parts of who you are— your roles both now and in the anticipated future.

2. How would you apply what you learned in answering the first question to your ministry to youth who experience same-sex attraction?

3. In your own words, how you would you describe the dominant narrative that exists around same-sex attraction today?

4. What are some practical steps you could take to help a young person develop a meaningful counter-narrative?

7

ON NOT HIKING ALONE: SOCIAL SUPPORT AND RELATIONSHIP BUILDING

A COUPLE OF YEARS AGO I WAS ASKED TO TEACH AN intensive course in Denver, Colorado. I was there for a week, and in my off-time, I drove up to an isolated spot in the mountains to hike. If you have done much hiking, you know that it is not always wise to hike by yourself. You never know what can go wrong. A freak storm, a slip on the trail, or suddenly getting lost. All I could think about, as I hiked the mountain paths, were those episodes of *I Shouldn't Be Alive* that I had seen.

As youth are navigating the terrain around questions of sexual identity, the same rule applies. It isn't wise to hike alone.

Unfortunately, for many youth, sharing their same-sex attraction involves great social and emotional risk. I've talked with countless people who have been told by leaders of local churches not to tell anyone about their attraction, which only confirms a young person's sense of shame.

Experiencing same-sex attraction or having a homosexual orientation often leads a person to experience isolation. Telling another person can change all of that. Although most disclosures begin with friends and peers, it is not all that uncommon for a student to share with a youth minister as well. Perhaps you've had this experience and have had a student in your ministry share about their same-sex attraction. Realize that this was a really big step for them.

Thankfully, there are examples of positive experiences that some youth have had in sharing their experiences. One young man said:

> One of my good male friends from my youth group—we started being accountability partners and I really felt like I was being dishonest by sharing everything but my same-sex attraction and so a couple weeks after I told my youth pastor I told my friend that there was something I wanted to talk about. (I had alluded to same-sex attraction before.) So one day he stopped by my house. It took me about a half-hour to tell him, but I finally told him.[52]

This young man was looking for a person who he felt could be trusted with this information. Sometimes a person finds that sense of safety when there is mutual transparency. In this case, the young man sensed that it was inauthentic to share his struggles with his friend without sharing this aspect of his life as well.

At this time of disclosure, people often ask sexual minorities who identify as Gay: How long have you known? Many of them will say, "I've always known." Skeptics reply (or at least think): "How is that even possible?" Parents often say something like:

"I've known you since you were born, and you've never done anything to suggest you were Gay! What about that girl you dated last year?!"

I would suggest that the first way to respond is by listening, and when appropriate, conveying to the person who has shared that she is not alone. This is true in at least two ways. First, let her know that she is not the *only* person who feels this way. There are many teenagers who struggle with their experiences and feelings of same-sex attraction. They don't know where to look to find information, or who to ask, or what to believe.

The second way you can communicate that she is not alone is by reminding her that all of us develop sexually. This process may not be exactly the same as what she is going through, but most people go through a process of sexual development and experience some type of shame, guilt over choices they make (sexual behaviors), possibly silence from their parents or mentors, and confusion about their religious identity and how their faith fits with the desires they have. Every Christian struggles to find God's will in forming their sexual identity. Again, there are differences for sexual minorities, but it is helpful to remind them that they are not entirely different by identifying common ground. Point out that all of us struggle in the process of understanding ourselves and our sexuality.[53]

Students may have heard negative comments about homosexuality in the church. This is a difficult portion of the trail to navigate. A church can teach a doctrinal position on sexual morality, but having a doctrinal position isn't the same as talking with someone about their same-sex attraction. In particular, we need to avoid the error of assuming that all those who experience same-sex attraction or identify as Gay think and act the same way.

For example, consider what it is like for a 13-year-old to hear that "homosexuality is a sin" without any discussion of how people bear the image of God, how all people are people of value and worth. How would you hear this if you also had strong feelings of attraction to the same sex? What if you had never heard of a distinction between attraction, orientation, and identity? What if you never knew that there were many examples of Christians who shared a Gay identity but made different choices about their sexual behavior? When people do not know that there are diverse responses, they tend to conclude that attractions are synonymous with behavior and identity. Again, a more careful discussion of these nuances is needed.

Sometimes teens will share with people they assumed would listen to them, including their youth minister, but they are told they need to "stop it," "choose differently," or that they "aren't trying hard enough." These tend to end the conversation. When people respond this way, some teenagers will decide that they don't want to consider other options for their identity and quickly move to expressing themselves through behavior.

At times, it may be appropriate for a youth minister to initiate a conversation, but this has to be handled carefully. What you don't want is to go all "Katie Couric" on someone in your youth group. You may recall the highly publicized interview Couric had with Manti Te'o, the sought-after football recruit from Notre Dame. As he was being interviewed by Couric about the hoax involving his "nonexistent" girlfriend, Couric alluded to the suspicion some felt that he might have fabricated his girlfriend to hide questions about his sexual identity. Couric put the issue out there in a rather blunt question:

> Couric: "One of the theories, many theories, Manti, making the rounds, is somehow you created this whole scenario to cover up your sexual orientation. Are you Gay?"
> Te'o: "No, far from it. *Far* from that."

My point is not to speculate about what Te'o's response means. I simply want to point out that direct questions like this are not always the best place to begin a conversation on this topic.

I know of one youth pastor who was new at ministry and thinking about its application to sexual-minority youth who made this mistake as well. He approached someone he thought might be gay and assumed that a direct question was a good way to start. Though he thought he was being pastoral and caring for the person, his question came across as confrontational. He questioned the guy: "Are you a homosexual?" I don't know too many 15-year-olds who are going to respond well to that approach. This youth pastor would have also done well to understand that bringing up the topic of sexual identity in this manner can end up introducing labels and categories that were not previously being considered. In other words, a student might think: "Well, if they call me Gay, then maybe I am." Others may feel hurt by the direct question yet continue to choose to identify with other parts of themselves besides their experiences of same-sex attraction. Again, you have to be aware that there is no such thing as a typical response.

In any case, choosing to tell or not tell is always a key dilemma for sexual-minority youth. For some, telling another person can be very freeing because it means that they are not alone in carrying that "burden" anymore. Yet for others, it makes them incredibly anxious because they are certain that if they tell someone, the response will be negative. How do you minister to a teen who's told another person and has had a bad experience? Let's say, for example, that a student has told his parents, but they did not listen and instead reacted with anger, disbelief, or rejection. If this has happened, first remember to listen, and if appropriate, clearly communicate to him that he is not responsible for how his mother or father reacted. You might also remind him that you understand that he did not wake up one day and choose to experience same-sex attraction. You can let him know that you understand it was not his goal to make life difficult for his parents. Offer to walk with him as he processes his parents' reactions. Continue to explore the relationship between his attractions and his identity and behavior in light of his Christian faith.

It is critical for you as a youth leader or volunteer to understand how important parents are in the life of youth, particularly youth who are navigating their sexual identity and their Christian faith. Sometimes a parent will react out of confusion, and this can quickly be expressed as anger, disappointment, or frustration. But an *initial* emotional response is rarely a longstanding emotional response. Some parents react out of grief: They grieve what they hear as lost dreams—the hope that a son will marry or a hope for grandchildren. I will cover this in more detail in chapter 8, but, in my experience, it is not uncommon for parents to react to a disclosure out of confusion or anger because they privately wonder if they have done something wrong. They may feel like they haven't done enough as a parent to foster a different experience of sexuality or sexual development. The reasons for this vary considerably, but parents are naturally protective of their kids, and they are quite willing to blame themselves as they look for an answer to the perplexing question: "Why is my son Gay?" Some may have heard that the cause of homosexuality is faulty parent-child relationships. This message—which is not supported directly by good research—can end up increasing feelings of shame in parents, who then direct their negative emotions toward their son (as anger, rejection, etc.).

Most teens choose to tell someone who isn't a parent *before* they tell their parents so that they have a better idea of how another person will react to the news. This can include youth leaders, pastors, coaches, teachers, siblings, and friends. It is most common for a teen to tell a friend.

You may be ministering to a teen who is weighing whether to tell a friend or parent. Although it's hard to predict how the person a teen tells will react, here are some potential benefits to sharing about experiences of same-sex attraction:

- They will not be alone—they may find others who love them to journey with them.
- They may find a great listener.
- They may find tools or resources that are encouraging.
- They can vent their thoughts and feelings instead of "combusting" on the inside (e.g., think can of soda that's been shaken).

On the other hand, there can be some negatives to sharing, particularly if the person is not understanding and decides to use this information against him or her:

- This knowledge can be used to blackmail an individual, or as a threat to manipulate them.
- Sometimes people respond with a set of expectations that are unlikely to be met (for example, "Well, you have to stop that nonsense!").

Hopefully, the person they choose to share with will be able to speak truthfully and fairly with them about their same-sex attraction without making unrealistic demands. They will try to see the challenges this student is facing through her eyes and with an appreciation for how difficult it is to share this.

RELATIONSHIPS

Sharing with another person raises related questions about relationships. These questions come up for sexual minorities and for youth pastors alike. Relationships are everywhere. Whether we see them as "good," "close," "distant," "cut off," "nonexistent," or any other descriptions, we are innately wired to be relational. One of the defining characteristics of human beings is that we have been created to be in relationships with others.

Relationships can be wonderful, but they can also be bittersweet. From a ministry perspective, we often talk with youth ministers who wonder how they can speak to youth who may be attracted to other youth. A teen may experience feelings of attraction to or feelings of arousal (i.e., "butterflies in the stomach") in their interactions with someone. This can be exciting, and can feel good at times. But that arousal can also be confusing or frustrating if it means that there are parts of the relationship that are "off limits." Consider the story of Jared:

> Jared grew up as an only child who tended to be more sensitive compared with other boys he knew in his neighborhood. His father tended to travel frequently for business, and as such, he became very close with his mother, and was never really known by his dad. In high school, he noticed that he was always drawn to the "jocks," particularly those who were not just athletic, but also smart and funny. Jared was a little frightened by the intensity of how much he wanted to be with one guy in particular, Matt. Matt was a wrestler who was also captain of the debate team and an incredible actor who frequently played the leading role in the school's plays. Jared had a couple classes with him and got to know Matt a little when they were randomly paired up as lab partners. The more he got to know Matt, the more he liked him and wanted to spend time with him. However, Jared freaked out when he suddenly had a random thought about wanting to kiss Matt and to let him know that he just really, really liked him.

Hearing Jared's story, you might be inclined to focus on his feelings of same-sex attraction. But this is about more than that. At this point, it is unclear exactly what his feelings for Matt "mean."

The first thing I would encourage Jared to do is to remain calm. Don't freak out! Affirm that he is not "weird" and avoid putting other labels on him. While it is important for him to accept that he has experienced attraction to another person of the same sex, this doesn't mean that these are *sexual* attractions, nor does it indicate that he has a homosexual orientation or a Gay identity. Secondly, I would encourage Jared to examine what it is that draws him to Matt. Is he just naturally attracted to people who are more beautiful or competent or intelligent? What is it, more precisely, that he is attracted to? Is it his athletic physique? His humor? His brains? Does he feel a need for Matt's approval? Does he want Matt to hold him? Or does he need to know that a guy like Matt could like a guy like him? The point in sharing this story is not to come to a conclusion about Jared, it is to simply point out that there are many directions you can go with what Jared experienced.

As someone who works with youth, try to remain calm when a student shares something like this with you. You will need to avoid freaking out, and you need to help the teen avoid that as well. Remember that the person you are talking to developed these attractions for any number of reasons. There is likely some combination from Nature (maybe they received a "push" in this direction) and Nurture/environment. Whatever the case, the person you minister to is attracted to certain types of people for *understandable* reasons, even if we do not fully understand what those reasons are at this time. Your role is not to figure it all out yet; you are simply assisting them as they figure out what to do about it.

Though I've said this several times already, it bears repeating: Keep in mind that just because someone experiences same-sex attractions or has a strong homosexual orientation, it doesn't mean that the person is Gay (as identity). It doesn't mean he has to act on what he feels. It just means that he experiences same-sex attractions—nothing more at this point. Before he makes any major decisions, it's important to understand more about these attractions. You can ask him what he makes of the feelings he has. Is it okay to appreciate that another person is attractive?

Is it more than that? If so, how so? Is there a desire to know the person better? Would knowing that person meet needs for closeness? Can he talk about that?

Some of the teenagers you are ministering to might feel uncomfortable thinking about these questions. But understanding more about the types of people he is attracted to and why he is attracted to them can really help him understand his experiences better. In turn, it can really help him make good decisions about the path he would like to take in the future.

Obviously, there are many questions that can be asked, and there are even more answers that can be given. You will want him to explore these questions . . . as many as he needs to. By wondering, he is confronting his fear instead of running away from it. He is exercising *awareness* of how he feels, what he thinks, what his opinions are, and so on, about same-sex attraction. Being more aware (or mindful) of his attractions can help him to understand what's going on inside, which helps him to make better choices about what he wants to do in response.

DEVELOPING FRIENDSHIPS

Some teens I have worked with say that they feel like they're alone, and that they aren't sure how to develop close, healthy friendships with other kids in youth group or in school because they are afraid that the other person might find out about their feelings of same-sex attraction. This is understandable. Most of us are afraid of rejection, especially if we think the other person may look at us unfavorably. This fear is real and valid. Junior high and high school can be difficult socially, and no one wants to be a target of teasing, ridicule, or harassment.

As a youth worker, you want to convey to sexual-minority youth that there are people who will not reject them. If there are friends she considers "safe," help her to see that such a reaction is probably not as likely. When a "safe" person finds out about her experiences of same-sex attraction, they are unlikely to forget about other "parts" of her identity.

ON BEING SAFE, ON BEING REDEMPTIVE

Let me comment on the use of the word "safe." This is language that comes from the mainstream gay community. It is used to convey an affirmative response to a gay person by a person who is considered safe. There are many ways in which creating a safe environment is discussed to protect sexual-minority youth.

Safety is important here. I've seen too many kids teased and bullied in youth groups, churches, and private Christian schools. I also sometimes think of the kind of environment I want to foster as both safe (emotionally, physically) and redemptive (spiritually). In other words, redemptive space (perhaps as a different way of thinking about safe space) is not only about protecting kids from abusive language, gay jokes, or bullying, but it is also going to emphasize the worth and dignity of the person before God.

Friendships, too, can be redemptive. They are one of the primary means by which God provides us with encouragement and support, and often that encouragement and support is in the direction of growing in our walk with God.

Also, you can convey that while these feelings of same-sex attraction may be on the forefront of her mind at times, whether she is feeling aroused or excited about someone, or whether she is anxious about someone finding out, we want to encourage her to consider that these feelings do not have to be all-consuming. That is, they do not have to swallow her up and define her completely.

One practical way to help young people navigate their sexual identity is to help them name and identify the different parts of who they are. You can help them see their identity in terms of their relationships and roles: as a student, a brother, a daughter, a friend, an athlete, a debater, and so on. In the same way, we want to encourage young people to consider feelings of same-sex attraction as a part of themselves (rather than treating their own feelings as toxic). Why? Because we want them to understand that these attractions do not have to be the first or most important part of who they are. They are still considering how much weight to give these attractions relative to the other things that define their identity.

There may be some teens that you know who claim a Gay identity, who say that they are defined by their feelings of same-sex attraction or by a sexual orientation that is directed toward members of the same sex. But remember, this is a choice they have made. Instead of arguing with them, you can ask them what this means to them. Don't assume that you know what their beliefs and values are about sexual behavior. That's another discussion.

The guiding principle in these conversations is the idea that youth are more than their feelings of same-sex attraction, as important and meaningful as those feelings may be. Remind him that none of us can be defined merely by our attractions, and that there are many people in his life right now who share his interests, values, ideas, and passions. He may be friends with some of them, or they may make great friends for him in the future—if he decides to reach out to them. The bottom line is that it is possible to connect with other people and develop healthy friendships with them *regardless of his feelings of same-sex attraction*. He can connect with them for any number of

reasons—shared interests, shared values, shared beliefs, even just having fun together!

So, for example, if a young woman in your youth group is interested in theatre, this might be a great outlet for her to meet other people who have the same interests. She may find some wonderful friends there. Or, if she loves sports, encourage her to join a team. Individuals who experience same-sex attractions need to discover that they can have relationships with others for reasons apart from their sexual feelings.

As a youth worker, you might be asking yourself, "Do I really want a teen in my youth group to be friends with other people who have same-sex attraction?" Keep in mind that all of your teens are developing their capacity to be in relationships with others. You'll find that some of these students will be attracted to others from time to time. They will need guidance from you and others in how to be friends when attractions and arousal may be an issue.

Positively, a person who experiences same-sex attractions may be able to encourage another because of their shared experience of same-sex attraction. However, we have also known young people who say that these relationships made the feelings of attraction more intense at times because this became the focus of their interactions together. Consider, for example, two people who have received failing grades on an exam. They may share their feelings of anger, disbelief, and fear with one another. While it may be comforting to know that there's someone else who also failed the exam, their conversations can end up intensifying their emotions. If this is happening with two students in your group, it would be good to talk with them about it.

One of the things you can focus on is helping students to understand what healthy friendships look like. How do you encourage healthy friendships among the students in your ministry? Here are a few characteristics of healthy friendships:

- They are mutually supportive—that is, both people feel that they are able to be listened to, heard, and that the other person values their thoughts, feelings, and opinions.
- They are honest—one person can share what is going on inside and the other person feels like he or she can do the same.
- They are real—both friends feel like they can be who they are without putting on any masks.
- They are not exclusive—they may have a circle of close friends or even a "best friend"; however, there are other people they call "friends."
- They are not defining—they are known as more than just the "friend of _____" and their friend is known broadly also.
- They are respectful—neither friend is critical or degrading of the other person.

Healthy friendships take time to build. Someone you minister to may be struggling with this, lacking the patience to build these types of relationships. Sometimes people who are "hungry" for a sense of connection with others will tend to tell "too much too fast" and "spill their guts" to another person. While this may seem like a good idea at the time, it can sometimes scare the other person off. So help your students to understand that relationships need patience.

In the formation of relationships, people typically explore a large breadth of topics before they "go deeper" and share more intimate details about themselves. So it is normal to begin with surface-level conversations and experiences, then gradually move to deeper topics and more intimate shared experiences. It's important to hold back in the early stages, to avoid telling the other person "too much too fast." Why? Because we want to know that the other person is going to be respectful of our trust before we share more tender and important details of our lives with them.

For example, if Sarah shares with Jennifer that her parents divorced when she was three, Jennifer may not be prepared to respond to this level of relational knowledge. If Jennifer bursts out laughing and makes snide comments or judgmental statements, Sarah might feel as though it is not safe for her to share other pieces of information with her, such as her attraction to other females. However, if the relationship develops to the point where Jennifer listens empathetically and carefully, Sarah might eventually sense that Jennifer is able to handle some of the more delicate parts of her story.

Relationships provide us with new perspectives as we reflect parts of ourselves to others. We find support and encouragement that lets us know that we are not alone. We value relationships because they make our lives richer. Think of all the times you have shared a moment of hilarious fun with another person. That moment wouldn't have been the same if you were alone. In the same way, sad moments aren't as sad when we experience the comfort and support of sharing them with someone who cares.

Henri Nouwen, a former Catholic priest and writer, once gave a description of a true friend. In his book, *Out of Solitude,* he writes:

> When we honestly ask ourselves which person in our lives means the most to us, we often find that it is those who, instead of giving much advice, solutions, or cures, have chosen rather to share our pain and touch our wounds with a gentle and tender hand. The friend who can be silent with us in a moment of despair or confusion, who can stay with us in an hour of grief and bereavement, who can tolerate not knowing, not curing, not healing and face with us the reality of our powerlessness, that is a friend who cares.

CHECK YOUR COMPASS

1. Ask yourself these questions: What would be the benefits of sharing my experiences with someone I trust? What would be the risks of sharing?

2. In your ministry, how do you foster greater intimacy and transparency among your youth?

3. When you encourage teens to talk to one another, how is encouraging personal transparency balanced against sharing "too much too soon"?

4. How do you talk with all of your youth about the friendships they have, and what guidelines do you offer when attraction and arousal are present in a friendship?

8

COMMUNICATING WITH BASE CAMP

PEOPLE WHO DO SERIOUS HIKING—HIKING THAT involves scaling the face of a mountain or ascending an icy peak—need to set up a base camp. When we think about this journey of sexual identity, the base camp represents the parents of the students in your youth group. Parental involvement is a necessary component of this process. Parents are essential to the well-being of the young people to whom you minister.

Just as a base camp is essential to a successful climb, having good relationships with parents is important to the development of an adolescent. Many of the young people we have surveyed said that homosexuality was not talked about in their family. The perception of most of the sexual-minority youth we talked with was that families were either closed to the discussion or essentially silent on the matter. This lack of conversation sets the stage for difficulties and conflict when communication about a topic no one is comfortable with eventually comes up. One person we interviewed shared this experience with us:

> I don't remember it being discussed; I remember hearing hints of it. I don't remember any full discussion of the issue. I just remember having an understanding that it was not a lifestyle that God intended for us to live. It probably came up at church when talking about Sodom and Gomorrah. I don't think my parents had any deep understanding . . . I was never really bold enough to ask probing questions b/c that might give me away.[54]

Not talking about homosexuality sends a message—that discussing it is off-limits. But this approach leaves older children and adolescents to learn about homosexuality from other sources, from media and entertainment, from their school, and from their peer group. That's not to say that what they hear is necessarily inaccurate or wrong, but as we have seen, all of this creates a storyline about how they can make sense of their same-sex attractions. They are looking for a storyline that is emotionally compelling, rather than a story characterized by shame.

Youth ministry staff and volunteers are in a unique position to help both the adolescent and the parents. It's worth the time to study and learn about this topic so that you can make it accessible to parents and to youth. You might give them some resources to read, but even more than resources, there is a point where *how* you interact with youth will be the primary method of teaching. Let's consider some common scenarios.

DISCLOSURE

In this first scenario, you become aware of a teen's same-sex attraction but the parents do not know. Keep in mind that this is something for the teen to share. It is best if the disclosure of information comes directly from the teen; however, you can work with him or her to prepare for that discussion, and you might even offer to be present. One way of beginning the conversation is to present the three-tiered distinction between attraction, orientation, and identity that I shared earlier. This can be a good starting point that can help some teens begin talking with their parents. Outlining these distinctions creates a way for a teen to describe what they feel rather than jumping to conclusive determinations of identity.

A teenage girl might say something like this: "Mom, Dad, I have something that I want to share with you. It's something I've been dealing with now for several months (or years) but have not known how to talk to you about it. I've not really understood how to think about it. It's been confusing to me. Ever since I went through puberty I have found myself attracted to other girls rather than boys. Like I said, this has been confusing for me, and rather than figure this out all on my own, I really wanted to bring you in, to know that you will support me as I try to make sense of it all."

This disclosure presumes a few things. First, it presumes that the young person is comfortable describing what she feels, rather than embracing her attractions as her identity. That may not always be the case. After all, our culture commonly treats attractions, orientation, and identity as one and the same thing, so they may be coming from that frame of reference. If you have had the opportunity to share the three-tiered distinction, and it resonates in some meaningful way with the student, she may be able to use this distinction to disclose to her parents in a more descriptive manner.

With Christian parents, it is particularly helpful to disclose experiences of attraction while one is not engaging in same-sex behavior. In one study we did, we had a young man share how his disclosure to parents, and especially his decision not to engage in same-sex behavior, seemed to help when it came to being transparent about his experiences of same-sex feelings:

> At first they took a deep breath. They were calm and troubled, but glad I was not engaging in it and acting out. They were understanding and tried to show me unconditional love . . . which is something I am grateful for. They were apologetic and put some blame on themselves, but we are still talking through that.[55]

Sometimes the disclosure is the result of a discovery, when a discussion occurs because parents suspect that their son or daughter is gay. They may come across pictures and messages in various social media groups that lead them to suspect their daughter's Gay identity. Then they initiate a discussion out of discovery (of a Gay identity) rather than disclosure from the student. A discussion based on discovery is often far more heated than the scenario I presented.

We have found, after multiple studies of Christian sexual minorities, that among those who chose to share their experiences with their parents, the typical age of disclosing is around age 17. Some young people share that their parent's response to them has been closely tied to "recovery" or "healing" or "change":

> They see me as . . . good . . . they see me as recovered in leaps and bounds compared to others who struggle with homosexuality. They are very proud of me. . . . I am using my past to help others.[56]

Others who have not shared with their parents wonder how their parents would respond. One young man discussed how he thought it might depend on what he said about his same-sex attraction:

> I'm not quite sure. If it was something I struggled with and was trying to overcome they would look upon that more favorably than if I said, "Hey mom and dad I'm gay." I used the

word accept. They would accept the struggles, but instead of the word accept they would be more supportive, in helping to get past this hurdle. . . . it would lead to some pretty serious consequences. . . ."

Others shared with us some of the challenges they have faced when parents do not trust them or otherwise are quite negative or critical. For example, one young man shared the following description:

> They are very mistrustful. Think that every relationship I have with a man is sexual. They treat me as an ex-felon . . . waiting for me to mess up. I was a good kid, now I am met with mistrust and expected to fail. They view me as going out with men to have sex, drinking, and partying.

Still others reported deep divides with their parents, even in cases in which their values appeared to be similar. One young man shared the following:

> Since family found out it has been very ugly. I told my parents because I don't think it is condoned by God. So trying to gain support, I told my parents. Parents did not treat me well after that. I told them to try to help change the struggle, but they think it is my fault . . . they stopped pursuing a relationship with me. I told them five years ago. Parents were my best friend and now they don't show any interest in my life whatsoever now.[57]

DAMAGE CONTROL

Sometimes the storm hits when you are scaling the side of the mountain. In these situations, you need to quickly move to safety and avoid further danger. If there has been family conflict over a discovery or a disclosure and you are called in to help with the situation, you will likely be engaging in some form of relational damage control.

One of the most helpful things to keep in mind is that parents have many feelings they need to talk about as well. When their teen discloses same-sex sexuality, the discussion can turn to questions about Gay identity or a gay description of orientation. But behind the discussion itself are a host of emotions and feelings. Some of the feelings are positive and some are negative. Positive feelings include love, care, regard, fondness, and loyalty. Negative feelings include confusion, disappointment, shame, guilt, fear, and anger.

Here is the first key to helpful ministry in these situations: *ambivalence.* Ambivalence refers to the ability to hold conflicting feelings at the same time. Parents are almost always ambivalent when they learn through discovery or disclosure about their child's same-sex sexuality. They have *both* positive and negative emotions toward their son or daughter. They may present as though they are one way or the other, but that is rarely the case in my experience.

The second key to help you in ministry is *polarization.* This occurs when one parent will primarily carry and reflect the positive emotions they both have toward their child, while the other parent will carry and reflect primarily the negative emotions they both carry toward their child. Keep in mind that both parents carry these positive and negative emotions—it's more a matter of which emotions they present to their child.

Youth ministers need to understand the reality of ambivalence and polarization so that they can avoid getting caught up in the "dance" between the parents, who may get into conflict with one another. As is often the case with Christian parents, one parent may not express her part of the polarization out of fear or deference to her partner and his strong emotions. Ministry entails drawing out the range of feelings they have for their child—both positive and negative emotions.

You, as a youth worker or minister, may also find yourself drawn to one side or the other when parents are polarized. At this point, you want to avoid allowing yourself to get too drawn into taking a "side" at this point. Rather, you want to help them appreciate the range of emotional responses they are having and move toward one another. If you side with one against the other, both parents will actually dig in more to defend their position.

Practically, when I speak with parents I name ambivalence as a common, normal experience. Then I explain what it means and alert them to the risk of polarization that can come with it. I ask if they have seen any of that in how they have been dealing with the disclosure or discovery up to this point. I might share an example of a couple who went through a similar experience and struggled with polarization, to give them permission to share their struggle now that they realize how common it is in these circumstances.

EDUCATION AND MINISTRY

As you engage in damage control, you are beginning to provide education to parents, helping them to identify and name both ambivalence and polarization. Next, you want to help parents come to a better understanding of what we know and do not know about sexual identity and orientation. The two most common questions that parents ask are: (1) *What caused this?* and (2) *Can it be changed?* Sometimes, along with asking about the cause of these attractions, a parent will ask a third question: *What did we do wrong?*

To answer the question, "What caused this?" I suggest being open about the fact that scientists do not really know at this point. There are many theories and not much by way of conclusive research. You can explain that some of the complexity about this issue is often reduced to Genes versus Personal Choice, but that these positions are caricatures of the discussion, part of the culture wars. Scientifically, sexual orientation does not appear to be genetic in the way we would think of something like eye color or hair color. At the same time, we know that it is not just a matter of personal choice. People find themselves feeling attraction toward the same sex.

A slightly more nuanced view of the debate is the Nature versus Nurture discussion. Unfortunately, this simplified division isn't all that more helpful than the Genes versus Personal Choice debate. Instead of being a choice between Nature or Nurture, it is far more likely that *both* Nature and Nurture contribute to sexual attractions and orientation, and that these contributions likely vary in strength from person to person.

I mentioned a question that parents commonly ask: What did we do wrong? You want to be sensitive to the parental tendency to blame themselves for their son or daughter's same-sex sexuality. This tendency can lead to shame for the parents, which can lead them to isolate from others in the church. This is a shame that is somewhat unique to the evangelical subculture, similar to the shame we discussed earlier. Again, remember that the formula[58] for shame involves (1) standards, rules, and goals; (2) the failure to live up to those standards; and (3) personal shortcoming that are the reason for the failure.

If we apply this formula to parents whose son has just come out as gay (even if he is not adopting Gay as an identity), we find a family that see themselves as having broken the standards for being a "good" evangelical family. Many ministries, in an attempt to combat the position that sexual minorities are "born that way," teach that homosexuality is the result of poor parent-child relationships that lead to emotional needs becoming sexualized at puberty. This ministry teaching provides the fuel for the last piece of the shame formula, leading to the conclusive result: The parent's personal shortcomings are the reason for their son's homosexuality. Now, in addition to the challenges they face coping with their son's disclosure, they must deal with their own feelings of shame for having caused his condition.

Parents react to this shame in a number of ways. Some withdraw and isolate themselves from their church community. They do not want to be asked how their son is doing. They don't want to lie, but they also don't want to talk about it. Isolation is a common, protective response, but it is not sustainable; isolation further exacerbates the shame they feel.

Others pray for God to step in and change their son. What parents experience is somewhat similar to the experience of the teenager who takes the same approach: If the parents pray and ask God to remove their son's attractions or take their son to a ministry with the expectation of change of attractions, they may soon find that there is not as much success or healing as they had hoped for. This can further confirm in their minds as parents that they (as parents) have not lived up to the standards, rules, and goals of the Christian community.

What happens next is often quite critical for the future of their relationship, both with their child and with the church. Some teens choose to adopt a Gay identity and turn to the mainstream gay community as an act of resilience. They find that the Gay-identity script provides them a way out of the shame associated with failure (not living up to the standards of the Christian community).

In a similar way, parents may make the same choice and decide to stand with their son or daughter. Some feel like it is an all-or-nothing decision, so they stand with their son or daughter out of the love they feel for them. If their son adopts a Gay identity and pursues a same-sex relationship, the parents must decide how they will respond. Some "agree to disagree" about matters of sexual ethics, which sounds easier than it often is, once you factor in dating, special occasions, adoption, and all of the situations that arise in relationships. Others change their theology to match the level of support they wish to provide (or they hold it as a point of tension at least—perhaps not with certainty either way). They may do this to survive the shame they feel. Sometimes this leads them to cut themselves off from those in their own faith community who represent a threat to their emotional survival.

As we bring this chapter to a close, let me offer you a summary of what I want you to take away from it.

Parents are really important in the lives of the sexual minorities in your youth group. You may be able to help your teens by facilitating a healthy, descriptive disclosure of the reality of same-sex attractions, as well as the desire to have parents become a source of support and encouragement. This is tricky; parents often struggle with a mixture of positive and negative emotions as they learn about the challenges their teen (and now their family) is facing. This ambivalence can lead to polarization. Being aware of this can help you help them prevent polarization that detracts from much-needed support. Be prepared to address questions about causes of same-sex attraction (*we don't know*) and whether they (the parents) are to blame (*no, they are not*). Do not underestimate the shame parents may experience within the evangelical Christian subculture. Be available as a resource to them, as they will need support, too.

CHECK YOUR COMPASS

1. What makes parents so important in the lives of teens who are navigating sexual-identity questions?

2. How might Christian subcultural shame affect a parent's ability to be supportive of his or her teen?

3. How would you describe the relationship between ambivalence and polarization to a concerned parent?

9

FINDING GOD ON THE TRAIL

THERE IS NOTHING LIKE GETTING LOST ON THE SIDE OF a mountain. Even if you aren't a believer in God, getting lost in the wilderness can get you to pray! My wife and I were once participating in a think tank that met in Lourdes, France. I was busy "thinking," so she and her friend took a rail car to the top of a mountain on the outskirts of the city. Even though their driver indicated that he would wait for them to return, soon after they began hiking they heard his bell ring signaling that he was leaving. Hurrying back, they found that he had left them, alone! (As an aside: If you are hoping to draw more tourism dollars to a region, do not leave people on the side of mountains.)

My wife and her friend instantly realized that no one was coming back for them. They were going to have to make it down the mountain by themselves. They tried to get the lay of the land and make a plan, but they also spent a fair amount of time in prayer. Alone and lost, they felt an acute need to have God present with them.

When people are navigating difficult terrain, they often ask the question, "Where is God in all of this?" There are many different reasons for why people feel what they feel. You could minister to teens who wonder, "Why do I have these feelings?" Unfortunately, there may not be an answer to their question. Experiencing these attractions and not having solid answers can lead to anger and frustration—at themselves, at their parents, and even at God.

If you minister to sexual-minority youth who have grown up in the church, then it can be confusing for them to hear condemning messages about homosexuality. A teenage boy in your ministry may have heard it taught that "homosexuality is wrong" and that it's a "sin." Hearing this can be really confusing to them when they begin to experience same-sex attractions. Your student may say to himself, "After all, I didn't choose to experience these attractions—they just sort of happened. How can something like that be 'wrong' or a 'sin'?" Hearing something like this at church may make him feel like there is something "wrong," "bad," or "sinful" about him. It may even make him feel as if *he* is bad *as a person*. He may even feel like he is "bad" *as a person* because he experiences these attractions. If so, he will be experiencing a great deal of shame and guilt.

To complicate things, he has likely heard people in the church, perhaps in his home as well, making insulting comments about gay people. They may have been made to him directly (as in, "Stop acting gay" or "You look like a queer"), or they may have been said within his hearing ("Guys who cry are Gay" or "Girls who dress like guys are lesbians"). When he hears comments like this from people who are important to him (parents, friends, teachers, coaches, and church pastors/leaders), it is especially hurtful. They may know that he experiences same-sex attractions, or they may not—but either way, it leads to further shame.

When talking with young people who are dealing with questions and conflict over their sexual identity, it's important to convey to them that this doesn't mean they are "bad" or that there is something "wrong" with them. Just because they have experienced a feeling, it does not make them an evil, horribly bad person. Emphasize to them that we *all* experience various feelings and struggle with different desires. Some people wrestle with feelings of envy or jealousy, while others struggle with eating or body image.

Still, even though you can offer some encouragement to a young person, he or she may still feel like there's a larger question: "Where is God in all of this? After all, if God thinks same-sex attractions reflect the fall, why did he allow me to develop them? And why doesn't he help me deal with them?" On one hand, she may feel like these feelings of same-sex attraction are a very large part of her, demanding all of her attention and mental and emotional energy. On the other hand, she may feel like she is isolated in the experience of these feelings because she has heard the message that "homosexuality is wrong," and she is afraid to share that she has feelings of same-sex attraction. This may lead to her hiding this aspect of her, shutting it down and stuffing it away.

All of this can be pretty confusing. It may lead her to feel torn—believing in God, knowing that she has same-sex attractions, and yet also believing that God does not approve of homosexuality. It can feel as though there is an impossible split between her faith and her sexuality. But it doesn't have to be a choice between one or the other. If she believes in God, it is helpful to invite God into this process of sorting out her feelings of same-sex attraction. Her faith can help her to understand what these feelings mean and what she can do with them. Some people feel comforted, less isolated and alone, and may have greater clarity about who they are when they invite God into the process.

COUNSELING TIPS

How does a teen invite God in? By being honest with God in prayer. "God, you know that I have feelings of attraction for other guys. How would you have me understand these attractions? How would you have me understand myself in light of what I feel? How would you have me understand myself in light of Your Word?"

Besides inviting God into the process through prayer, it can also be helpful to think about what God's intention was for human sexuality—that is, looking at the bigger picture. When it comes to feelings of sexual attraction (not just those who experience same-sex attraction) and how those translate into sexual behaviors, it is helpful to look at the purpose of these sexual attractions. What, according to God, is the purpose of sexual attraction and behavior?

If you belong to a church or a religious institution, you have likely been taught that God intended sexual intimacy to be experienced in marriage between a man and a woman. There are many different reasons for why this is taught and accepted:

- The vulnerability of engaging in sexual intimacy is preserved in marriage, which is a committed relationship.
- Sexual intimacy is an emotionally, relationally, and physically bonding experience that is devalued if it is treated as a casual activity.
- Sexual intimacy was created for males and females to

experience with one another—for pleasure in addition to procreation.

- Sexual intimacy between a man and woman in marriage is meant to teach us something about God's love for his people, the church—so sexual intimacy is tied to something beyond any two people and their behavior.

A young person might ask you, "So, where do same-sex attractions and sexual behaviors fit into God's intention for sexuality?" After all, same-sex behaviors may be just as arousing and just as stimulating as sexual behaviors experienced between people of the opposite sex. But what does God *intend*? It can be helpful to talk about how a man and a woman who have sex outside of marriage *just because they can* are not participating in God's vision and purpose for sexual intimacy. In other words, if sexual activity occurs outside of God's plan of a covenantal marriage between a man and a woman, then it is outside of that plan, regardless of sexual expression or attraction.

At this point, teens are likely to experience several different emotions, such as frustration, discouragement, confusion, anger, and sadness because they see that their feelings of same-sex attraction are being contrasted with God's intention for sexuality. It's important to ask questions and to acknowledge how this feels for them. There should be no pressure to change their sexual attraction so that they can get married to someone of the opposite sex. While I know of people who have told us that they have experienced these kinds of significant changes, it is important to know that this is not a common experience. I believe it would be a mistake to talk about it as an expectation for the person to whom you minister.

As you minister to a student, the real issue is not what they should do if the feelings toward the same sex do not go away. Instead, highlight the tension that people who have same-sex attraction feel because they have an understanding that sex—

according to Christian tradition—is reserved for a man and woman in marriage. Many people, at this point, have wished that their feelings of same-sex attraction would just "go away." Some have prayed for a long time that God would just "take away" those feelings; however, they still remain. This leaves them in a state of frustration and anxiety. Some people wonder if they are "praying enough" or "working hard enough" and they end up feeling badly about themselves. Other people feel angry with God because they feel like he has not heard their prayers. Maybe a teen you work with has had similar reactions. If so, you can encourage them with the idea that this is a process. Talk about how he feels now, what he currently understands, and how the way he thinks about it may be different years down the road. There are many things that we go through as we mature and grow older that help us to become the people that we have been created to be. Part of this journey is learning how to deal with difficult things and learning not to give up in the midst of very painful parts.

What we are talking about here is the lifelong process of *sanctification*. It's the process of life and growth—the trials, the difficult times, the moments when we feel like we're at the end of our ropes—that spur us through the process of becoming more and more like Christ. You can talk about how, as Christians, we are saved by faith in what Christ has done for us, from the moment we say, "Jesus, I believe that you saved me from my sin." But it is also good to talk about how this is just the beginning. What follows our salvation is the process of working it out— becoming the person God has created us to be. As the popular saying goes, "God loves you just as you are, but he loves you too much to leave you there." Talk about how God wants to help us grow, to become more like his Son, Jesus.

You may have heard that to mold iron, it needs to be heated and there is a process of repeatedly striking it to form a new shape. In being sanctified—made more like Jesus—we are brought through a process of heating and reshaping so that we can be who God intends us to be. Dealing with same-sex attractions is not easy—hence the heat and the pain—but it is not without purpose. In this process of transformation, God is refining us to make us someone new. Feelings are being reshaped—feelings of jealousy, self-hatred, envy, and other destructive emotions. Desires are being reformed. As a person who ministers to youth, you want to help them come to understand that this is a day-to-day process that will lead them closer to God.

It is natural to feel like giving up on something that is difficult and time-consuming. I know that the practice time it takes to learn to play the piano can be grueling and lengthy, but I also understand that you don't play a masterpiece the first time you touch a keyboard. In the same way, while youth will want to quickly "get over" these feelings of same-sex attraction and be "done with it," they will need help from you to give them a long-term perspective. Remind them that we don't know why some people have these feelings of same-sex attraction and others do not. There are different reasons such as environment, temperament, and peer groups that may influence a person's experience. But just because we don't have all the answers, it doesn't mean they should throw in the towel and give up.

Underscore God's purposes in creation—his creational intent—in more general terms as well. You don't have to focus exclusively on heterosexual marriage, but on this more general idea: "The God who created me knows best how human beings will thrive." Remember that God is not surprised by the challenges they are facing. This aspect of trusting God has been very important in the lives of sexual minorities who decide to remain chaste. They decide to submit to God in the areas where it does not *feel* natural for them to submit.

In one of our interviews, we asked young people to share how their faith had helped them cope with their experiences of attraction. Several people shared how the conflict they felt pointed them to God's love for them, and that understanding God's love with greater depth had helped them cope. One young woman shared the following:

> My faith background has shown me, when I came out to my minister, that God loves me for who I am, it's actually helped me more than hurt me. It's given me something to strive for.[59]

Give youth the space and time to feel, recognize, embrace, and work through their feelings of same-sex attraction. And don't avoid God in these discussions. After all, having these feelings may be part of this student's journey to becoming the person he has been created by God to be. For some reason—unknown to us—this experience has a purpose. It might prove to be helpful to someone else in the future (e.g., reaching out to others and offering them comfort through your experience). Ultimately, it may be how God reveals himself to others.

Some teenagers have found the following prayer helpful:

> Heavenly Father, I would like to invite you into my experience. I do have feelings toward the same sex, and I want to ask you to be with me in what I am experiencing. Please guide me as I search for ways to respond to my feelings of attraction. I do not want to pretend that they aren't there, and I don't want to box them up. I want what I feel, my thoughts, my actions, and my intentions to be used by you, and so I ask for your guidance and direction.

This prayer might be the start of an honest and more transparent ministry for you as you minister to youth with same-sex attractions. It acknowledges—without shame—the reality of their experience. With this foundation in place, we now turn to some specifics: What does this actually look like in the day-to-day reality of youth ministry?

CHECK YOUR COMPASS

1. As someone who provides ministry to youth, what questions do you want to ask God about sexuality and same-sex attractions?

2. How do you think God feels toward the kids in your youth group who experience same-sex attraction?

3. What does a person's experience of same-sex attraction lead you to believe about God and his character?

10

MINISTRY BETWEEN MIRACLES

A FEW YEARS AGO I WAS SPEAKING TO A GROUP OF Christians about sexual-identity concerns. They came from a somewhat more charismatic background and were focused on healing as the primary way of responding to homosexuality. As I was trying to connect with them and share a little of my own perspective, I mentioned that I frequently pray for people when I minister to those who are hurting. Typically I do this in the context of the Life Group/Cell Group I co-lead or in our corporate worship gatherings, when people come forward to receive prayer. I told them that I believe in the importance of praying for our needs and the needs of others and that I believe God can both heal and provide for our needs.

To stretch the group a bit, I shared about a study I had conducted of people who had attempted to change their sexual orientation. This was a study we had recently concluded that tracked people for seven years through their involvement in Christian ministry. The findings had not been warmly embraced by either "side" in the culture wars. Those who were convinced orientation never changes did not like the results since we reported that some people did experience meaningful changes in attraction (along a continuum). At the same time, those who believe everyone who tries hard enough or has enough faith should expect complete change to heterosexuality were also not pleased with our findings. Few of those we surveyed reported this level of complete change, and those who said they had experienced a level of change acknowledged that they still had experiences of same-sex attraction at times.

I could sense that the group was trying to process the results, that I had challenged some of their assumptions, primarily that there would *always* be a dramatic change of orientation—a complete change from gay to straight. When I sat down, a man approached me and shared an idea he had encountered in a book he had read with the title, *Ministry Between Miracles*. This is a book written to those who come from a more charismatic background, encouraging them to consider the need for ongoing ministry and pastoral care on the front lines—the work that must be done in the days and weeks (or more) between the expected miracles. That's an idea I can embrace as well, and what I want to look at in this chapter. What is the ministry we do *between* the miracles that we hope God will do in answer to our prayers?

What is involved in this kind of ongoing care? In the previous chapters, I've laid a foundation for offering counsel to teens that involves talking about their feelings and dealing with their shame. In this chapter, I want to unpack some of this in more detail. What are some of the things to be alert to as teens talk? How do you help teens deal with the shame they feel?

To set this up as a constructive discussion, I find it helpful to begin by talking about conflict. I do not believe conflict is our "enemy." Rather, conflict within ourselves can provide us with important information for ministry and growth. When we quickly move to suppress, control, or avoid tension, we lose insight into what a young person feels inside. Conflict can be a great source of helpful information.

One productive place to begin with sexual-minority youth is helping them become more aware of their *emotional reactions*. This often begins with the internal conflict they feel. This conflict typically leads to negative emotions like frustration, confusion, or anger. Some internal conflict will shine a light on the relationship they have with their parents and with God. Other conflicts can be revealed by looking at the questions they have been sorting out. As someone who ministers to youth, you have an opportunity to sit with these youth and ask them about their expectations. What were they expecting from their parents, from God, or from others in the church? This can uncover some of the emotional needs they have and answer some of why they are experiencing conflict. These needs can then be named and cared for in a more intentional way.

Remember that your goal here is not to solve problems. You are sitting with them in the moment, letting them have a place to talk about what they feel. You are getting a better sense of their emotions and their needs, and this will inform you as you seek how best to help. Try to avoid bringing yourself into the equation as a solution to their problems—or worse, their conflict. Instead, seek to locate yourself outside of the conflict so you can help your youth come to a better understanding of what they are experiencing. It is important that teens avoid "shutting down" their thoughts and feelings. When they do this, their feelings will come out "sideways." In other words, when feelings aren't expressed verbally, they end up coming out in other ways, through indirect expressions that might not be healthy. A teen might yell at others (a sibling, parent), hurt themselves, or experience depression or anxiety. When we acknowledge our thoughts and feelings it does not mean that we act on them. It simply means that we are honest with ourselves and others.

Also keep in mind that teens are at a unique place in their lives. As teenagers, they are going through many physical and emotional changes. They have hormones raging through their bodies, which can make them moody and increase arousal (e.g., "feeling horny") and feelings of attraction. Sexual minorities are experiencing all of this as well; it just so happens that they have feelings for members of the *same* sex. Key relationships are changing in their lives, most significantly their relationship with their parents. For some teens, their friendships are also changing as they discover new interests that some of their older friends don't care about. Perhaps the teen you meet with is into punk and ska, and the friends she grew up with are into hip-hop. Also their minds are growing, and they are finding it easier to think outside the box than when they were younger. They are developing new connections in their brains that accompany these changes inside their bodies. Even their dreams are changing as they think about the future—dreams about what they want to do, and who they want to be.

In other words, this is a time of transition. And the kids you are working with are growing and developing in many ways. From their point of view, they want to have the chance to explore different parts of their identity, and this includes their sexual identity—who they experience themselves to be sexually.

COUNSELING TIPS

It can also be helpful to take note of feelings that a youth may have when she is thinking of, or is with the person that she is attracted to. By doing so, she is better able to choose what she wants to do with the feelings she has and what they mean to her so that she's not limited to one type of experience. For example, someone may receive the message at one point in her life that because she had same-sex attractions, she was automatically Gay. Unfortunately, because she may not have known there was an alternative, she may have automatically adopted Gay as an identity.

If you were meeting with a teen you might talk with her about her feelings of attraction. Perhaps all she knows for the moment is that when a good friend walks into the room, she just wants to be right there beside her, and she's not sure why or what that desire means. Some people experience a desire for emotional connection with a person, whereas others are drawn physically and sexually to that individual. Part of what is under consideration in your conversations is how their experience of same-sex attraction is unique to them.

CIRCLING BACK TO SHAME

In chapter 4, we discussed how shame is a negative emotion that results in self-condemnation and anticipates condemnation from others. Shame results when a person is raised in a community that teaches various standards, rules, and goals; that person perceives himself as not living up to those standards, rules, and goals, and he attributes that failure to personal deficiencies or shortcomings.[60]

How does a youth worker respond to this shame? I would like to suggest four layers of care you can offer to an individual: identifying shame, managing negative emotions, changing unhelpful thoughts, and helping her to be in healthy relationships.

Let's take a look at each of these.

First Layer: Identifying Shame

This involves helping youth recognize that they are dealing with shame in their lives. They must first understand what shame is if they hope to see it reduced. You can share with them that guilt has to do with feeling bad about something we did wrong. When we lie to our parents, we feel guilt. Similarly, we feel guilt when we don't do something we should do. If I am supposed to tell my friend that I cannot make it to lunch, and I fail to call him, then I should feel guilty about that.

But shame is different. Shame has more to do with how I feel—feeling bad about who I am and not what I've done. Shame says that there is something deficient *in* me. Shame says that if someone knows about this deficiency, they are likely to reject me.

In talking to a young person about shame, it can be helpful to compare and contrast it with guilt. It can also be helpful to talk about how *common* shame is among people who are navigating questions about same-sex sexuality. This is where it might be helpful for you, as a church leader, to take some of the responsibility on behalf of the church for the way in which we have dealt with this topic in our churches. It can be helpful to admit that some of the conversation in the church has likely contributed to these feelings of shame among people who experience same-sex attractions.

Second Layer: Managing Negative Emotions

This involves learning how to manage strong, negative emotions. Sometimes experiences are so distressing that the people we minister to can't even interact with others effectively. At times like this, we need to help them focus on themselves and getting back to a place where they are able to function at a basic level. This involves finding things that help people calm down, "self-soothing" behaviors that help them to soothe themselves from the distress they are feeling. Self-soothing behaviors can help to replace negative emotions like anxiety, fear, frustration, sadness, and lust with positive emotions like peace, security, contentment, joy, and love. There are lots of ways a person can soothe him or herself. Here are some self-soothing behaviors that are helpful to a lot of people:

- Listen to music.
- Play sports.
- Take a walk.
- Do something creative/artistic.
- Connect with others via social media.
- Exercise.
- Talk with friends.
- Read a book.
- Watch a good show on TV.

In fact, any activity that is helpful to that person and isn't harmful to them or to others is probably a healthy "self-soothing" behavior. The best activities are those the person enjoys—the ones that give her a sense of happiness and satisfaction. So ask her about those kinds of activities. Such activities will help to replace the negative feelings that were distressing her with positive feelings that will encourage her.

Unfortunately, there are also *unhealthy* "self-soothing" behaviors. Some of these include: taking drugs, drinking alcohol, smoking cigarettes, cutting or other forms of self-injury, isolating from others, looking at pornography, and overeating. Even some of the healthy "self-soothing" behaviors described above can become unhealthy if a person either: (1) Uses them to "escape" from the real world for long periods of time, or (2) Uses only one or two of them without doing any others and becomes dependent on them. In ministry, you can know if a healthy "self-soothing" behavior has become unhealthy because the behavior will start to hinder that person's life—affecting their schoolwork, relationships, and so on. If the person doesn't overuse them to escape and uses a variety of behaviors to cope, then they are probably doing okay.

It would be the "elephant in the room" not to mention masturbation at this point. Is masturbation an example of a healthy or an unhealthy self-soothing behavior? Let me begin by saying that this is a complicated topic that deserves time and attention, as well as balanced reflection. In one of the best resources I have seen on the topic of masturbation, Steve Gerali discusses it in the context of wisdom. What he means by this is that masturbation isn't always a black and white issue. It "could be sin for some and not for others."[61] This is not a cop-out answer. Gerali spends time carefully reflecting on Scripture, looking at various historical factors, as well as our current cultural context. Like other wisdom issues, this is a topic that requires Christians to search and study Scripture for principles that inform the decisions we make. As a youth worker or youth pastor, this is an area where you can be an encouragement to youth by being a resource they can talk to. You can model openness and transparency as appropriate behaviors, as well as fostering in them the desire to grow spiritually such that they can turn to the Holy Spirit for wisdom and guidance.

Part of what you will want to convey to young people who are stressed about navigating sexual-identity concerns is that whenever fear, stress, and anxiety seem to paralyze them, they do not have to give their feelings the final say. There are things they can do to calm down. The common reaction to such experiences is to give in to them and give up. They might start feeling sorry for themselves, feeling alone and as though they have no one to help them. In place of these, encourage them to find some healthy "self-soothing" behaviors that help.

Another strategy to suggest is that they "interview" their emotions. This involves confronting the distressing emotions they are experiencing and interviewing them, asking questions of them as if they were a person. This may sound odd, but for many people, it really does work to reduce their fear, stress, and anxiety. For example, one young man I know interviewed his sexual behavior this way—asking questions of the same-sex behaviors that caused him regret. He asked the question, "In what areas of my life have you been causing me problems?" His answer, "In my self-esteem . . . how I viewed myself and how I measured myself. Initially you controlled the parameters of my self-esteem. Fortunately, that is not the case anymore by the grace of God."

Sexual behavior can also change over time. The interview can include questions like, "In what areas do I seem to get the best of you?" One young man shared, "When I confess to a friend . . . the *acceptance* dampers the shame/guilt."

Third Layer: Changing Unhelpful Thoughts

This has to do with how a young person thinks about himself. Keep in mind that shame is the result of self-condemnation and the expectation that others will be equally rejecting, so that has to be addressed. From a ministry standpoint, the church needs to communicate that who we are is of great worth to God.

In a curriculum[62] developed to help people reduce shame, several suggestions were offered to facilitate this understanding of our worth before God. I have organized the core considerations that lead to shame, as well as what it has meant to redeem shame for many Christians who are navigating these concerns (see Figure 6).

You will note that the formula that leads to shame can be countered by some important claims made by Christians. But— *and this is critical*—these claims cannot be left as abstract declarations; they have to be lived experiences.

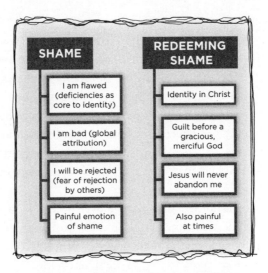

Figure 6. *Shame and Redeeming Shame*

First, we have an identity in Christ that is based on faith in him (Ephesians 2:10; Colossians 1:21-23). This counters the experience of deficiencies as core to our identity. While we are all fallen creatures in need of redemption, we recognize that God loves us and gives us value and worth by virtue of that love (Ephesians 1:7). So we may do things that are wrong and feel guilt for those choices; we all live our lives before a gracious and merciful God who understands (Hebrews 4:15). However, *we need to experience this reality in actual relationships with fellow Christians*, whose love for us manifests this belief in an emotional and spiritual encounter with God's grace and mercy.

In other words, we need communities of grace. Terry Cooper talks about how inadequate it is to make personal declarations of our worth apart from experiencing that worth in community:

> I do not think that any of us has the power to completely accept ourselves in isolation. Once the suspicion of inadequacy has set in, I cannot pull myself up by my psychological bootstraps and declare myself acceptable. The dark forces of rejection are too

powerful. . . . How does it help to "declare myself okay" when it is my own testimony that is on trial in the first place?[63]

When we do not experience the affirmation of God's love within the Body of Christ—with real people who know us intimately—the concepts remain too abstract to do most of us any practical good.

Christians affirm that Jesus will not leave us (Hebrews 13:5). This is an important truth that counters the fear of rejection. Here, too, this abstract declaration (that Jesus will never leave us) needs to be born out in real relationships in which others who profess the name of Christ do not actually leave us. That is, rather than rejecting us, they stay with us and provide us with love, encouragement, and support. God wants his church to be the living embodiment of his love.

I do not want to convey, however, that the other side of redeeming shame means that we are somehow free from pain. The redeemed side of the equation is also painful at times because we live in a fallen world and pain is a part of that reality. But shame can be reduced when it is countered by these basic truths and they are imbedded into a person's understanding and lived experience.

Fourth Layer: Developing Healthy Relationships

This brings us to the fourth layer of ministry: developing healthy relationships. This starts with their relationship to you as a youth worker. One way sexual-minority youth learn to deal with their distressing emotions is by talking with someone about their experiences. As a youth worker, you are going to be an obvious candidate. Adult youth volunteers may be the people who are first approached. So you want to be able to sit with and listen to people with a range of emotions as they share about the conflict they have. Often this alone can help them cope with their feelings.

Your relationship with a young person will help him explore and test his beliefs. He will learn that he is not deficient, that he is not worthy of condemnation, that others will stand by him. Sometimes young people will fall back into unhealthy patterns, returning to the ways in which they previously managed their shame. *Do not let this derail your ministry to them.* They may have a habit of isolating themselves (to avoid condemnation they deem inevitable). They may turn to defensive, even destructive, behaviors. It is important that you remain in relationship with them. By doing so you challenge the assumption that they are going to be rejected.

Depending on the time you have and your experience in this area, you may need to have the teen see a professional counselor or therapist. That person will be working on some of these same issues. They will also work with your teen on finding healthy ways to cope. You can aid in this as well. One thing a teen can also do is "step outside" himself every once in a while and help others in some intentional way. He might volunteer at his church, school, or in his community. "Stepping outside" can actually help him put his struggles into proper perspective. For example, if he is a volunteer who is working with children who have cancer, his struggles with same-sex attraction may not seem quite as difficult as they did before.

COUNSELING TIPS

A youth minister can also help teens identify the strengths implicit in whatever it is that makes them feel "different" or "other than." These would be strengths that set them apart from the crowd as unique and gifted. For example, we have known young men who were unusually creative and sensitive, whose gifts could be used to serve others in meaningful ways.

The following are some ways a young person could volunteer:

• Help tutor students at school who are having trouble in subjects he is good at.

- Volunteer at a hospital, children's ward, or retirement home.
- Serve in the Sunday school, children's ministry, or youth ministry at church.
- Volunteer at Habitat for Humanity, building houses for those in need.
- Help coach a children's sports team.
- Volunteer at a local soup kitchen or homeless shelter.
- Go on a short-term mission trip.

These are great ideas because they help him take his eyes off himself and help others, and, in some instances, they may capitalize on the "differences" that have been a concern to him.

It can also be helpful to talk with someone who has experienced same-sex attractions themselves and has learned how to cope with it. Of course, it's not always easy to find such people. As a youth minister, it helps if you have connections in the community, people who can be a resource in these moments who are able to share from their experience.

MAKING REFERRALS (OR DEVELOPING PARTNERSHIPS)

Any discussion of coping raises the question: What if the teen I am working with is not coping well at all? When do I make a referral or develop a partnership with a professional counselor? We know that sexual minorities tend to report more difficulties with depression, anxiety, and other unhealthy coping behaviors, such as substance abuse and nicotine dependence. So there may be good reason to partner with a professional counselor or therapist when these other concerns are part of what your teen is going through.

You can reflect on the issue and ask yourself questions that include the following:

- Although we all get down from time to time, does this person's depression seem to persist and is it interfering with their relationships or school performance?

- Stress and anxiety are not uncommon during the teen years; however, does the anxiety persist and disrupt relationships or performance at school?

- Keeping in mind differences in temperament and personality, has this young person withdrawn or been gone from youth group without explanation?

- Although any of our kids may turn to unhelpful ways to cope with difficulties in life, is there any use of drugs or alcohol?

- While it isn't uncommon for some teens to be moody and irritable from time to time, is there any discussion of suicide or self-harm?

When it comes to making the decision to refer, you want to talk to the sexual-minority youth about your concerns and listen to what she has to say. You begin with, "Let me say how much I appreciate you being part of the youth group. I'm glad you are here. Let me also share what I am seeing." Then talk about the signs of depression you see or the anxiety or the stress or the withdrawing behavior.

It can be helpful to normalize the issue as well as the referral: "I've known other kids over the years who have also struggled with depression at times, and they have gotten a lot out of talking with someone who works in that area. In fact, I know someone who I trust; someone who I think would be a good person to talk to."

Keep in mind that a referral works best when it is a partnership, when you partner with a professional counselor or therapist to serve the needs of your youth. Also, a referral to counseling almost always necessitates obtaining consent from a parent. You may be helping the teen talk to her parents about what she is feeling and why meeting with a counselor may be a good idea.

Before a young person talks to someone else who has gone before them in this journey, it is good to remind them that their journey may be unlike this story. Help them to remember that each person who has same-sex attraction deals with it very differently. If the person they talk with is older, it is likely that he or she has come to better understand his or her feelings and experiences through a variety of means, which may include prayer, individual counseling, therapy groups, conferences, books, conversations, and revelation. In other words, there is no "cookie-cutter" experience of journeying through same-sex attractions. What works for one person, may not work for another—and vice versa.

In addition, coping with same-sex attractions means that the young person needs to acknowledge that this is something he is going through. It's part of his reality. In a form of therapy called "Dialectical Behavior Therapy" by Marsha Linehan, there is a phrase she uses that helps people to acknowledge reality. It's called *radical acceptance*. In radical acceptance the person realizes and understands that these feelings of same-sex attraction are part of his day-to-day experience. To cope with this "unwanted" situation, he has to first acknowledge that it is there and accept that it is a very real part of his life.

When someone does not accept this, there are a few options that remain:

- They can try to change how they feel, but that's not something that we generally want to encourage. It means denying how they really feel about their attraction.
- They can try to change the situation, but if it is not changeable, it leads to wasted effort.
- They can choose to deny that their circumstance is real and be miserable. There aren't very many people who would want to feel badly for long periods of time.

Instead, they can choose to accept who they are and what they are experiencing. To illustrate, here's an example:

Let's say that you are at the beach with some friends, and you're out swimming in the water. Suddenly, you feel like you're being pulled out further into the ocean by a strong current called a riptide. What are your options? For one thing, you can choose to deny that you're in a riptide; however, you may be in trouble because you may be pulled out farther than you can swim. A second option is to fight the riptide and try to swim to shore. The probability of that happening is slim to none because riptides are very powerful, and even the strongest swimmer will wear himself or herself out without gaining any ground. The likely result would be that the person would drown. The third option would be that you could give up and say, "Oh well! Here I go!" and do nothing about it. So, the possibility with that option would be that you might get pulled out really far, or that you might possibly drown. The last and most helpful/hopeful option would be to acknowledge that you are in a riptide, accept it, and swim parallel to shore. That is the only way to survive that strong current.

Helping a teenager radically accept their experiences of same-sex attraction does not mean they are saying, "I'm Gay."

Radical acceptance of their feelings of same-sex attraction means that they acknowledge that this is part of life for now, and that it's something that they will continue to work through. There's always hope in radical acceptance, because transformation begins with acknowledging the existence of whatever you want to transform. Coping with same-sex attraction begins by simply acknowledging that the attraction exists.

There are a number of ways to cope with the things we struggle with in life. The important thing is to remember that as you encourage youth to use some of these activities or skills, do them because they are meaningful to them personally. Although distraction is also an important element of coping, it is not always helpful because it may lead to escapism, where someone may avoid dealing with their struggle altogether.

Here are a few ideas:

- Write about her story—that is, how she came to realize that she experiences same-sex attraction and what it means to her.
- Journal about some of the questions she may have.
- Put together a collage of pictures that represent who she is and the different parts of her. For example, things she likes, activities she enjoys, people who play important parts in her life, role models, things she would like to do someday, roles she participates in, and so on.
- Express this journey in a form of art—poetry, sculpture, a painting, and so on.

Regardless of your theological tradition, there is a need for basic ministry and pastoral care, even when it occurs between those times when we pray for the miraculous. I do not want to discourage people from praying for what they need in this area. But how we pray says a lot about how we view God, ourselves, and our circumstances.

I have seen some ministry casualties where youth have been led to believe that healing would be reflected in a complete and easy change from gay to straight. This testimony of change then becomes the measure of that person's spiritual maturity. But this is a misleading and risky message to send to young people who are navigating sexual-identity concerns. It is often justified with the rationale that those in ministry are giving youth "hope," and that they are "believing in big things from a big God." Experience suggests that this is the wrong path to head down. I have seen more damage done this way than healing, creating more shame than compassion.

Again, while some people have reported meaningful changes along a continuum of attraction, most people do *not* experience all that much change in the basic feelings they have toward the same sex as well as a corresponding increase in attraction to the opposite sex. Their expectations are high, but they don't experience what they hope for. This is not an indictment of God or God's power. Nor is it an indictment of that person's faith or their level of spiritual maturity. After all, what would you say to the Apostle Paul who earnestly prayed that God would remove the "thorn" that Paul viewed as a difficulty in his own life (2 Corinthians 12:7)? That thing, whatever it was, was never taken away in his lifetime. This ongoing struggle was not a reflection on God's lack of power, nor was it a question of Paul's faith or his level of spiritual maturity. Instead, it was a means for Paul to grow to learn to trust and depend upon God, even in the midst of a besetting condition.

If the only message we send to a teenage girl wrestling with same-sex attraction is that her testimony of healing and change must be a strong attraction to men, as evidenced in marrying a man and having children, we limit what God can do. There is also a testimony to be found in living faithfully before God in whatever state we find ourselves in. As those who minister the hope of God's grace to youth, let's agree to minister out of confidence in God, that he will provide for us what we need each step of the way.

CHECK YOUR COMPASS

1. What questions or concerns do you have about helping a teenager "unpack" his or her feelings of same-sex attraction, even if it is just to understand them better?

2. How would you respond to a youth who has been "shutting down" his feelings of attraction? What might be helpful in shutting down feelings? What might be an unintended consequence?

3. Are there any areas in your life in which the use of radical acceptance could be helpful? How would your personal use of radical acceptance inform your ministry to youth?

4. Can you describe several different testimonies of how God could be at work in the life of a Christian who experiences same-sex attraction?

11
MAPPING A MINISTRY FOCUS

BASED ON THE INTERVIEWS AND SURVEYS WE HAVE conducted over the years, I've concluded that young people today definitely want to talk about sex.

They want to be informed, and they want a place where they can be honest about the questions they have. In our work, we have asked sexual minorities about this, and they have repeatedly indicated to us that they wish this topic was discussed more frequently in their local churches. Since youth are thinking about sex, and many of them are already talking about it with their peers, you might as well jump in and have a voice in shaping the discussion!

To do this effectively, you can begin by reflecting on your own attitudes about sex. Your attitudes will be conveyed to youth when you speak about sexuality in general—you can't hide what you think. As someone who ministers to youth, you will convey your attitudes through the things you choose to talk about (and what you don't), how you talk about those topics, the questions you ask, as well as your nonverbal expressions. There will be helpful and unhelpful attitudes that you convey in your ministry. A helpful attitude might be that sexuality is a natural part of human experience, that it can be pleasurable and fulfilling rather than aversive or discontenting.[64]

This means that you should also have adequate sexual knowledge. Admit what you do not know, and consider who you turn to for good and accurate information as well as insight and consultation. Consider what you have personally experienced in your own sexual development and sex life. It can be helpful as you prepare to teach about sexuality to reflect on your own sex history so that you can better understand how life experiences impact you today. You may also gain some insight into the challenges people face in talking about sexual matters.

Reflect on how sex was discussed in your home growing up, what you were exposed to (in terms of modesty or nudity) in your home, how affection was expressed (verbally and nonverbally), as well as how you responded to changes at puberty. Think about your first dating experiences. Sexual experience includes but is not limited to struggles with sexual dysfunction. Perhaps you have dealt with addictions or sexual-identity concerns yourself. Whether you have or have not will inform your ministry to youth. If you have never struggled with any of these issues, that, too, can impact the ministry you provide, as sometimes our personal struggles increase our capacity to empathize with others.[65] If you are married, I encourage you to work on having a healthy, fulfilling sexual life together with your spouse. If you are single, I encourage you to be working on having a healthy sex life in the broadest sense of that phrase, by understanding your sense of being male or female (your gender sexuality), knowing your longings and desires, relating in healthy and meaningful ways with members of the same and opposite sex, and understanding how your behaviors express your sexual interests and values.

It is also important to understand that the feelings you have about your own sexuality and sexual expression can range considerably from comfort to discomfort, peace to anxiety, and from confidence to guilt or shame. Some people are remarkably comfortable discussing various facets of sex and sexual functioning. Others are notably shy and reticent to discussing anything having to do with sexual behavior. Most people fall somewhere in between.

Take care to consider what is appropriate with regard to your own self-disclosure, especially when speaking with youth. With knowledge of your own sexual development, how sex was discussed in your home growing up, and an awareness of your present attitudes and feelings about sex, you can be a great resource to the youth in your ministry. Teenagers want to have an honest discussion about sex, and *when it is appropriate to do so*, it can be helpful to share some of the questions and concerns you had at their age, as well as how you navigated difficult topics or experiences in your own life. But there is also a need for some discretion and the need to exercise wisdom.

There is always a possibility that the youth you are walking with in ministry will become attracted to you. This can be quite difficult for some who work with youth, but in these cases it is important to communicate a couple of things to them. The first is that they have not done anything wrong in having these attractions. They may feel especially shameful for having feelings of attraction for a youth leader. Let them know that it is not wrong for the young person to share those feelings with you. That in doing so they have taken a huge risk, and you can express your appreciation for their honesty and transparency. At the same time, you need to reiterate to them that this is a safe relationship—one that is safe because those attractions will not be acted on or taken advantage of. Try to avoid pulling away from the person, which may lead to increased shame. Stay engaged with them. Invite them to participate in meaningful ways in the youth group. Affirm them as a person. As with any expression of attraction, it is wise to set boundaries around the relationship. Avoid being alone with them or saying or doing things that could be misconstrued, but again, try to refrain from pulling away after a disclosure like this.

Unless you are in an unusual ministry setting, your ministry focus is likely to deal with sexuality in broader terms. Most youth workers will not be exclusively focused on sexual-minority youth. Much of your work will be with heterosexual youth and there may be sexual minorities in the mix. Some of the youth will be sorting out sexual-identity questions or concerns; others may not. This puts you in a good position to discuss sexuality broadly with students, and that's what I recommend. It is best if sexual-identity concerns are discussed in this broader context of healthy sexuality, not as an isolated focus. This allows you to normalize experiences by reminding your youth that a percentage of teens will experience same-sex *attraction* (4-7% of teens and maybe about 6-8% of adults) and that some will experience strong, persistent attractions in such a way that they would say they are *oriented* to the same sex (about 1-3%). Most of the folks with an orientation will end up adopting a Gay identity, but not all of them (and most sexual minorities we surveyed at Christian colleges did not adopt a Gay identity at the time we surveyed them). Most of those who identify with a same-sex orientation eventually engage in same-sex behavior as an expression of their identity. But, again, not all of them do.

As you minister to youth your goal is to expand options for them. In our cultural context many youth see attraction as synonymous with identity. From here they see behavior as an expression of their identity. As we have been discussing throughout this book, the issue is more complex than this simple progression. There is more to consider at nearly every step along the way. And you want your young people to grow in their own emotional and spiritual maturity so they can make more informed decisions about their identity and behavior.

As you discuss same-sex sexuality as part of a larger discussion about sexuality in your youth group, I want to outline some of the ministry perspectives "out there" that your students will be exposed to. It will be helpful for you to understand what these are and what their strengths and weaknesses are. The three perspectives are referred to as:

> Hope for Change
> Freedom for Identity
> Celibacy and Friendship

THREE MINISTRY PERSPECTIVES

It is probably fair to say that there are as many ministry approaches to the topic of sexual identity as there are ministries. In a study we conducted a few years ago, we tried to identify the exemplary ministry approaches to sexual minorities in the church. What we learned from this is that people tended to nominate ministry approaches that were pretty distinct from one another. The first type of ministry perspective emphasized healing of the sexually broken. That kind of ministry appeals to some people but not to others. The second kind of ministry perspective focuses more on welcoming everyone, but does not affirm same-sex behavior. Again, this is appealing to those who adhere to a traditional Christian sexual ethic but are not holding out healing as the expectation or standard for all who are sorting out sexual-identity concerns. The third type of ministry perspective mentioned to us was gay-affirmative. Perhaps as a response to the damage done to sexual minorities, some felt that the only option that remained was to be affirmative, even if that meant revisiting traditional understandings of Christian sexual morality.

In the years since conducting that study, I have found it helpful to organize what I see today in terms of ministry approaches into three broad perspectives on ministry: hope for change, freedom for identity, and celibacy and friendship. These do not correspond directly with the ministry approaches from our original survey, but they do reflect the most common and thoughtful approaches that I see on the ministry landscape for churches today. Each of these perspectives is rooted in a traditional understanding of the church's teaching about sexual morality and behavior.

Hope for Change Focus

A number of ministries have recently reasserted the importance of communicating that there is hope for change for those who have same-sex attractions. By this hope what is meant is that there can be real, meaningful changes in not only behavior but also identity (in Christ) and with regard to orientation and attractions. This is frequently framed as "change is possible," but it essentially conveys to people that there is hope that people can experience meaningful and substantive change away from homosexuality and toward heterosexuality.[66]

What is appealing to many people about this approach is that it corresponds to teaching about a "Big God" who can do "Big Things" as a result. Real hope exists because people believe that God can do anything.

One upside to this approach is that people want to hear a hope-filled message. If a person struggles with their same-sex attractions, a message that offers hope is initially a great encouragement to them.

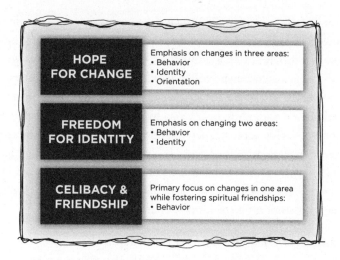

Figure 7. *The Ministry Landscape*

The downside of this approach is that fewer people actually experience the dramatic changes that are anticipated. What happens to them when their hopes are not met? People can swing to the other side of an emotional pendulum to a place of great confusion, frustration, or worse. "Failure" here is the kind of experience that can end up driving people toward a Gay-identity script if the lack of change or success signals to them that they really are a categorically *different* kind of person (Gay) than they initially thought.

Freedom for Identity

The freedom for identity approach tends to downplay the strong emphasis on changing attractions or orientation—though it remains open to the possibility of change. Instead, the focus is on finding freedom from having same-sex attractions become the defining features of a person's identity.[67]

While this seems to be a more mediating, realistic approach, it is still unclear exactly what constitutes "change" in this perspective. Is it change of orientation? Of identity or behavior? For many people in this area of ministry, freedom means that there is minimally a change of behavior *and* a change of identity. I would suggest that this approach to ministry is focused on finding freedom *from* behavior that then leads to freedom *for* a different identity.

What is attractive about this approach is that the ministry goals are more likely to be reached by more people. The goals are modest, so this approach can include those who wish to change their behavior through prayer, Bible study, corporate worship, and fellowship. All of this leads to the creation of new ways of behaving and thinking about oneself. The downside is that some feel it does not offer the kind of change they hope for.

Emphasis on Celibacy and Friendship

More recently, I have seen the growth of another perspective on ministry that places more of an emphasis on celibacy[68] and friendship. This perspective may have resulted from not experiencing the change that had been hoped for. Perhaps as a result, the focus is placed more on living a celibate life and exploring the meaning of spiritual friendships and community as a way to sustain that call.

It is unclear to me how this message will be received by youth, since our culture has an almost idolatrous obsession with romantic love.[69] To the extent that our culture equates romantic love with experiencing true happiness and fulfillment, young people will continue to hold out hope for change or some resolution that allows this as an expectation. They may even have a sense of entitlement, that they deserve this romantic fulfillment. If a person's ultimate fulfillment comes through having a spouse and children, is it any wonder that young people tend to feel "set up" or "robbed" if they do not have those things? This raises a good question: Can marriage be valued while we *simultaneously* value singleness? The church will need to make some adjustments if it wants to hold out celibacy as an expectation that is meaningful and fulfilling, rather than a burden.

HOW ARE THESE THREE MINISTRY APPROACHES RELATED?

As a youth minister or volunteer, how should you think about each of these three perspectives? Unfortunately, these perspectives often end up competing with one another. I would encourage you to avoid picking a side here. In fact, one could argue that all three approaches have merit, that none of them are the final or only way to minister to people. It may very well be that we find that each is part of a larger developmental process of responding to the conflict between sexual and religious identities. We may learn that some are a better match for specific people based on their experiences, theology, and personal temperament.

The truth is that most people who experience conflict between their sexual identity and their religious identity at some point do ask God to help them by *removing their attractions* to the same sex. In other words, they ask for healing. This is the focus of the first ministry perspective. So the truth is that most people start there.

It might help to view these different perspectives as a funnel, and know that most of those who hope for change will likely not experience the dramatic change they hope for. They face a critical, vulnerable time in life in which they may reject the Christianity they see behind the "hope for change" ministry model. They may adopt the Gay script and believe that this other trajectory (toward gay identity, same-sex behavior, the mainstream gay community) is the best way to respond to unmet expectations.

Others, however, will reevaluate their expectations over time. What they may find is that participation in ministry leads them to freedom (from behaviors they wish to discontinue) that in turn provides them with freedom for identity. This identity is frequently discussed as an identity "In Christ," which is often viewed in this ministry model as incompatible with a Gay identity.

And even among this group, not everyone will resonate with this outcome or with the ways in which the ministries here talk about a person's behaviors, attractions, orientation, or identity. They may find a home with the more recent approaches which some see as an alternative to the focus on orientation and identity change. They may wish to identify as a celibate gay Christian.[70] Although this may not appear to be a ministry movement, like we see with the other approaches I've described, as individuals, these folks tend to be more visible or "out." The upside of this approach is greater access to support through existing friendships. These individuals are less likely to look to parachurch ministries that focus on "contending" against a "struggle." They are conservative Christians with regards to sexual morality, but they have come to terms with their same-sex sexuality as a part of their lived experience and, in many cases, as part of who they are as a person.

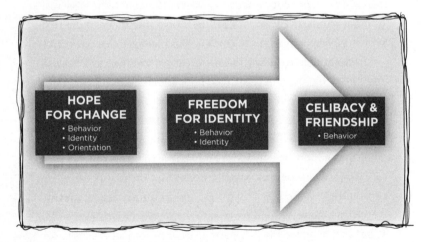

Figure 8. *The Ministry Landscape as a Process*

So for many reasons, these folks are more comfortable using the word "gay" to describe themselves. They experience their same-sex sexuality as a distinct part of who they are as people. What is different about them, as evidenced in their same-sex sexuality, is also seen in their temperament or personality or in their creative impulses. Still others evidence this distinction for gender-related reasons—where the experience of being male or female does not always fit into the cultural expectations or stereotypes we have for masculinity and femininity. They may not see these differences as deficits. When people respond to them by saying, "But it's wrong to form your identity with your attractions," they miss the point these individuals are trying to make—that their sexual impulses are not the sum of how they experience themselves as "different."

What has stood out to me in my interactions with celibate gay Christians is their interest in developing meaningful friendships and communities that would support their celibacy. In keeping with this emphasis on celibacy and spiritual friendships, while celibate gay Christians may want to improve relationships with their parents or other significant people in their lives (or resolve the negative emotional consequences from childhood sexual abuse), they do not assume that this resolution will make them heterosexual.

I know some celibate gay Christians who introduce themselves as a gay Christian, essentially saying, "If you care to know more about what that means to me, I'll be glad to discuss it with you." Others, like Wesley Hill,[71] will typically say, "I am a celibate gay Christian." Here they are letting the other person know that they (likely) subscribe to a traditional Christian sexual ethic. But they do not want to be part of a larger cultural debate that they see as steeped in contradictions and wordplay. You might ask, "What about hope for those Christians who identify as celibate gay Christians?" Wesley Hill illustrates this point well:

. . . calling oneself a "celibate gay Christian" may be a way of *expressing*, not giving up, hope—but expressing it in a way that doesn't link that hope to orientation change. Claiming the label "celibate gay Christian" means, for me, recognizing my homosexual orientation as a kind of "thorn in the flesh." When the apostle Paul used that phrase in his correspondence with the Corinthian church, he made clear that his "thorn" was indeed an unwelcome source of pain (2 Corinthians 12:7). But he also made clear that it had become the very occasion for his experience of the power of the risen Christ and, therefore, a paradoxical site of grace (2 Corinthians 12:8). Paul, I think, would have had no qualms about labeling himself a "thorn-pricked Christian"—not because he recognized his thorn as a good thing, in and of itself, but because it had become for him the means by which he encountered the power of Christ. Likewise, living with an unchanged homosexual orientation may be for many of us the means by which we discover new depths of grace, as well as new vocations of service to others.[72]

The challenges that exist for the "celibate and friendship" model (and to some extent the freedom for identity approach) is that there is a need to develop the kinds of communities that can actually support celibacy. This is a broader question for pastoral care for all who are single, but there are unique challenges that face sexual minorities that should not be glossed over.

WHAT HELPS AND WHAT HURTS?

We have asked young adults to share what has helped and what has hurt as they have moved to a place of forming their sexual identities. I have been impressed by how same-sex relationships meet the emotional needs of people—even those who do not eventually adopt an identity as Gay. For example, one female we interviewed shared:

> People I was attracted to were my best friends. Whoever I was close to, they became my object of attraction. . . . The hardest thing was my realization that I was leaving a person behind. It wasn't just sexual.[73]

Others just did not have examples they could follow; they didn't know anyone who was walking this out. For still others, unwanted sexual experiences complicated questions about sexual identity. One young man in a study we conducted shared the following: "My uncle's molestation . . . I had to put love and sex together because of that. I had to accept that someone would love me and want to have sex with me."[74]

Another person who ended up not identifying as Gay spoke of how his faith made the difference: "My faith. That was the first thing that encouraged me to change. God was powerful enough to pull me out of it."[75] Another man spoke more of how same-sex experiences were ultimately not fulfilling to him: "How dissatisfied I was with it when I really embraced it. My lover didn't fulfill what I needed . . . it was just sexual desire for me, not a connection that I was seeking."[76]

ON "VICTORY"

I was talking recently with a friend of mine who is in youth ministry. He shared that he feels good about the way the youth group is inviting of all kinds of kids. He has worked hard to create an inviting, grace-filled atmosphere. The challenge, he said, was in helping kids who experience same-sex attraction find "victory."

"We pray together and these kids will be really sold out for Christ. They are actively engaged in our worship together. I meet with these kids and minister to them. I know that they want victory. They go after it hard. But even after many months, they seem to be still dealing with homosexuality. I don't know how to coach them to a place of victory. They may not be in a same-sex relationship; they may not act on their feelings, but they still have the attractions. One guy said to me recently, 'I just don't know how to be attracted to a girl.'"

"In your church culture," I asked, "How is victory defined?"

"We would say that a person has victory over same-sex attractions when the attractions go away, when the person has heterosexual attractions," he said.

"What would it be like in your church culture, in your youth ministry, if victory were talked about more in terms of growing in Christlikeness?" I asked. "What if sanctification was the primary focus, rather than the current focus you place on changing their attractions?"

"I don't know," he shared honestly. "That's not the way we've thought about it."

"What I'd like you to think about is whether placing so much emphasis on change of attractions ends up putting more pressure on these kids and on their expectations for the specific ways God should be working in their lives. In my experience, while some kids may end up experiencing some movement either away from same-sex attractions (and in some cases toward attraction to the opposite sex), most will likely not experience as much change as they had hoped for. So, while you don't want to discourage them in that, I think it might be helpful to frame 'victory' around the kinds of things God promises to each of us—that he is committed to bringing us further along in spiritual maturity, in Christlikeness, and I wonder if there is room in your ministry for that to occur independent of whether attractions change. It seems to be a more attainable goal, and I think there is less risk of shame. I wonder about whether those expectations for victory end up making the kids feel like it is either their fault for not having victory, or that it is God's fault in a way that makes them want to give up on their faith altogether."

"Yeah, I see what you're saying," my friend said. "I don't know how that would be received. That's an interesting shift, and I can see why it might be important. But why wouldn't God bring the kind of victory we talk about?"

"I don't know," I admitted. "But I do know many people—folks a little older than the teens in your youth group, who have talked about their same-sex attractions as more a part of their life as they know it. Some might say it is like Paul's 'thorn in the flesh'—something they asked God to take away, but they still have it. They have tried to find meaning and purpose in it; they have tried to find ways to bring glory to God through it.

"Others have talked about their same-sex sexuality as a distinct part of who they are as people. They see themselves as maybe more creative and able to relate to different kinds of people than others might. Some are what we might describe as gender atypical, by which I mean their experience of being male or female does not always fit into the cultural stereotypes we have for masculinity and femininity. They very well might not experience these differences as deficits. Some might still wish they had attractions to the opposite sex, but they have come to terms with their attractions in a way that has led to some peace, some resolution in their heart. I don't know that they would use the language of 'victory' to describe that resolution, but maybe that language would resonate with them."

As you think about setting a ministry direction in a way that lets you speak into the lives of sexual-minority youth, let me offer a few practical recommendations for ministry.

1. Teach and Model a Curriculum of Sexual Stewardship

Young people today want to talk about sexuality, and they are already talking about it to some extent. You can be part of shaping that discussion, so think about a Christian sexual ethic and how you want to communicate that ethic to young people today. I believe that any teaching on matters of sexual ethics should be well thought out and framed around a positive view of sexuality. So rather than teach narrowly about homosexuality, it is usually better to speak more broadly to a Christian view of sexuality.

What I have found helpful is to introduce to young people the biblical concept of stewardship—seeing ourselves as being responsible for those things we either have been given in this life or otherwise experience in this life. The principle of stewardship can be found in a number of passages throughout Scripture. For example, Matthew 25:21, in which the person who is faithful over a few things will be made faithful over more; 1 Corinthians 4:2, where we are encouraged to be found faithful; and 1 Corinthians 6:19-20, in which we are told that our body is a temple that we are to take care of.

In the church today, most discussions about stewardship are limited to what it means to steward our finances or maybe being a good steward of the environment. Youth may resonate more with the application of stewardship to the environment, as there has been a generational shift in how we have prioritized taking good care of the local and global environment, in addition to concerns regarding social justice and the distribution of material goods. So I find that to be a good place to start. They can talk about ways in which they are good stewards of the environment, and they can acknowledge when they have not been good stewards of the environment. The things that they do (or do not do) tell a story about who they are in relation to the environment.

Once teens grasp the principle of stewardship, it can be

extended to the area of human sexuality and sexual behavior. In matters of sexuality and the desires and impulses we may feel, it will be important to steward what we experience in our desires and impulses. What I like about this principle is that it applies to everyone in the youth group—those who are attracted to the opposite sex and those who are attracted to the same sex. If the youth group leader and volunteers are married or single; each of us stewards our sexuality.

Put differently, a key consideration for stewardship is that it is not dependent on the state a person is in. The message to single Christians is not "Steward your sexuality until you get married," as if stewardship were code for practicing abstinence or part of a larger *"Just Say No"* campaign. Rather stewardship is for those who are single and those who are married.

Stewardship reflects a call for all of us to honor God with our sexuality, as our sexuality is not ours to begin with, but rather is one of many aspects in the human experience that is ultimately God's, and we can find ways to honor God through our sexuality and its expression.

There is also an important opportunity to talk about singleness in a way that truly values it. Too often we treat being single as an incomplete state for the Christian. When we are not intentional about valuing singleness we may send the unintended message that marriage is preferred, and that will add pressure to sexual minorities to pursue heterosexuality as a way of being accepted by the local church.

This message coincides with what is said about healing and freedom. Those outcomes are needed if the only way to be in the local church is to be married (heterosexually) and have children. Another direction to go is to hold more realistic expectations (if they want their attractions to change/diminish), and to value being single—whether a person is attracted to the same or opposite sex.

2. Create Redemptive Space

Eugene Peterson puts it well: "Our membership in the church is a corollary of our faith in Christ. We can no more be a person and not be in a family. It is part of the fabric of redemption."[77]

We need to be part of the larger Body of Christ. We need community. But we need to make certain that the local youth group we are a part of can be that community. If young people are exposed to silence on the topic of homosexuality or gay and lesbian issues, they will draw the conclusion that homosexuality is so bad it cannot be discussed. Or if they only hear about condemnation, they will set up an "us versus them" mindset in which they locate themselves as part of the out group. Either of these scenarios leads to shame.

It is common in the mainstream gay community to talk about creating "safe places." I tend to think of this more in terms of creating "redemptive space." I mean by this a community that allows for and fosters greater authenticity and transparency for the purpose of pursuing and being pursued by God. No more jokes or language that is at the expense of youth who are navigating sexual-identity issues. If someone says, "That's so gay!" or "Stop acting queer!" take time to talk about what might be conveyed in those expressions, as well as possible unintended consequences. These are important teachable moments. It will be difficult for a young person to approach you about sexual-identity questions or concerns if the words that are spoken by others (and ensuing silence by leaders) communicate to her that it's not okay to be transparent.

One young man spoke of how name-calling affected him: "In high school, I was called 'homo,' 'fairy,' and 'fag' because I was in gymnastics and theatre."[78] Another young man had a similar experience: "I overachieved to show everyone that though I was different, I was still acceptable. My peers had a lot to do with my self-image. If you're called 'homo' or 'fairy' for five years straight, you start to believe it."

Of course, avoiding language like, "That's so gay!" is only the beginning. All of your youth will benefit from you modeling how to engage this difficult topic. They have Gay friends, and they may know good friends who are navigating this terrain. They, too, need help in becoming a good friend to someone who is sorting out these issues in their lives. The principles that have been outlined in this book would be part of that teaching and modeling.

I have suggested in several places throughout this book that it is important to distinguish between politics and pastoral care. The church has to stand above the culture wars in terms of being able to minister to the needs of those within our communities who are navigating this terrain. That does not mean we are released from our duty to be responsible citizens who participate in local and national discussions about political matters. However, much like articulating correct theology, if we believe passing laws will be sufficient for practical ministry, we are sadly mistaken.

Toward this end, you might consider adopting "convicted civility" as your ministry brand. As you consider any highly volatile topic under discussion today, consider approaching it through the lens of convicted civility. Clarify and communicate what you hold as your convictions, and convey those convictions with respect for others.

Extend the brand of convicted civility to what it means to be compassionate. To feel the questions and concerns of the other, the person we may find it hard to believe that God loves. When it comes to young people in our own communities who are sorting out sexual-identity questions, we do this to improve the climate in our communities so that we do not further isolate them.

AN ATMOSPHERE OF GRACE

In terms of setting an atmosphere, let me share how one youth pastor[79] I know has set out to establish a culture of grace. This came about after a hard lesson. The previous year he had thought he had things pretty well set up in terms of having a welcoming atmosphere. A young person came to visit the youth group, and the leader went up to talk with him, make him feel welcomed. The guy was fairly effeminate in how he carried himself and spoke with others. After welcoming him and chatting for a few minutes, the leader had to attend to another issue. He was away for only 3-4 minutes. When he returned, he couldn't find the visitor. He asked after him, but was told he left after a really bad exchange with some of the other guys in the youth group. They had apparently teased him and maybe even confronted him about how he was coming across, and the kid left. Why stay where you feel unwanted?

This experience was a wake-up call to the youth pastor. He felt a burden to be more intentional in training his staff, including shepherds, leaders, and grade captains. He needed more people who would buy into the idea of setting an atmosphere of grace.

The first thing he pointed to was that the church's lead pastor was also purposeful in changing the atmosphere in the larger church. That was being set by how the pastor talked about people and concerns, and the ways in which he was personally and appropriately transparent about ongoing challenges in his own life. The lead pastor had been working with the staff and volunteer leadership in the church through monthly workshops/trainings to help them be better prepared for a wide range of people who would be drawn to an atmosphere of grace.

As far as the youth group is concerned, the youth leader has shepherds, leaders, and captains. Shepherds are the adult volunteers who work with the youth. He has grade-specific, gender-specific shepherds who work with the various kids. He then designates leaders. These are high school seniors and older who lead small groups that meet during the various breakouts. These leaders are treated as part of the youth group staff. He also has captains. These are grade-specific leaders, so he is talking about 8th-grade, 9th-grade, 10th-grade captains who are "undercover" leaders. They are taught leadership principles and philosophies, and he has found that one of the best ways to make these principles concrete for everyone is to talk through specific case examples. They meet together to go over any number of case studies of situations that could arise, such as public displays of affection, new visitors, disclosure of abuse, and so on. *How would you respond in this case? What if another kid spoke up first and was not being as gracious?* In other words, he has them thinking through and discussing together the kinds of encounters that are critical to fostering an atmosphere of grace.

In one of his lessons, he talks with his team about the lone red Legos. He is referring to his own childhood here, and he remembers being a kid who couldn't allow any of his Legos to be all alone. If he saw a lone Lego, he would have to stop what he was doing to find another Lego and join them. He talks to his leaders about how important it is to be on the lookout for the kids who seem to isolate themselves or who are isolated by others. He would train them to search for them and connect with them. He shared with me that many of the lone red Legos in his ministry have been sexual-minority kids. Whether they keep an arm's length from others, or if others end up rejecting them, they are often on their own.

An atmosphere of grace is set not by changing theology regarding sexuality and sexual expression, but by how we discuss these topics, as well as how we relate to one another. It has to be modeled by the leadership of the church. It has to be taught in very practical ways. And it has to be practiced daily.

3. Reframe Your Discussions

The place to begin is to think of Christians who are navigating sexual-identity issues in adolescence as "our people." What I am referring to here is a story I've told many times of listening to two gay psychologists talk about how the mainstream gay community had failed "our people" by not meeting their spiritual needs. They were talking about how gay people would leave the gay community to participate in Christian ministries that these two gay psychologists ultimately believed were harmful to gay men and women.

I genuinely respected and appreciated the deep compassion these gay psychologists showed for people they felt a strong connection to. What saddened me that day was that I had not heard a Christian leader say anything like that. No one I knew in ministry was saying, "We are failing 'our people'" in terms of not supporting young people who are navigating sexual-identity questions. But compassionate ministry starts here—with recognizing that Christians who are navigating this terrain are "our people."

Recognize, then, that Christian sexual minorities have been exposed to two primary scripts: a Gay-identity script and a script that has led to shame. The Gay script is emotionally compelling, as it answers questions about both identity and community—critical answers to normal developmental questions asked during adolescence. The script that leads to shame is steeped in silence and condemnation of the person who experiences same-sex attraction.

As I have been suggesting throughout this book, compassion toward sexual minorities means this: that there are young people (age 14 or even younger) who first experience same-sex attraction at around the time they go through puberty. They "find themselves" feeling attraction toward the same sex. Those experiences may be confusing to many of them, particularly in light of being raised in a Christian community that does not tend to talk about homosexuality or talks about it in a singularly negative way that may end up contributing to a sense of labeling and shame for the youth.

As I indicated in the opening chapter of this book, we have relied too much on orthodoxy as if the intellectual defense of sexual ethics was sufficient to say we have discharged our responsibilities for pastoral care. While the church should not change its teachings on matters of sexual morality, we have to change the assumption that correct teaching functions as pastoral care in its entirety. We can and must do more—and it begins by recognizing how our culture has created a sense of meaning, purpose, identity, and community that is tied to same-sex sexuality.

I suggested that some people have found it helpful to distinguish between attractions, orientation, and identity. This allows people to be honest about what they feel (attractions or orientation) without necessarily jumping to identity and corresponding behavior. This should not be used as a weapon, however. It is meant as a pastoral resource for those who are able to make these distinctions and find them helpful as they navigate this terrain. Some sexual minorities will reject it out of hand and teach that there is no conflict between same-sex behavior and Scripture. Other sexual minorities will feel perfectly fine identifying themselves as gay as shorthand for their same-sex sexuality, but they will refrain from any same-sex behavior. Still others will not feel drawn to that identity label, even if it is merely adjectival.

I have shared that the primary script that many young people are familiar with is a gay script that collapses real differences between attraction, orientation, and identity, so that experiences of same-sex attractions can at times be treated as synonymous with gay identity. Other scripts need to be identified and developed, but they have included things like an "in-Christ" script and a "post-gay" script.

I also think it's important to communicate realistic biblical hope. This has to do with what is said about "healing" and "freedom" from homosexuality. This will likely vary by denomination and other assumptions held in various theological traditions. However, when pastors convey a kind of "arrogant optimism" about healing and freedom, it can have unintended consequences. While the pastor may want to build hope and faith, what may happen is that the young person feels more shame and anger if he does not experience the kind of healing and freedom he was led to expect.

So the question to ask yourself is: If I throw out the word *hope* to the people under my spiritual care, where do I expect it to land? If we expect hope to land on orientation change, by which most people have in their mind complete change from gay to straight, then we have a problem. The church already fosters a climate in which we pretend to be better off than we really are. So any suggestion or expectation that orientation will completely change puts people at risk of living a life of some deception, a life lived behind a mask.

If you throw the word "hope" out there and expect it to land on Christlikeness, then I think we are heading in the right direction. When hope lands there—on the expectation of sanctification, we are trusting in God for something we know with certainty he has already promised to fulfill.

Along these lines, it is important that as young people "story" their lives, they learn to create a "future story" that they are moving toward. As a youth minister, you can help teens think and explore ways in which their gifts, passions, and creative abilities can be used to shape the world in ways that give them a sense of meaning, purpose, and calling.[80] You want to help them dream big here. What kind of vibrant life can they experience when their gifts and passions are brought together in service of the Kingdom? You want to start thinking *life trajectory* here, and you want them to begin to see how their current choices are linked to that "future story" they are moving toward. Part of the realistic biblical hope that you are instilling (that is often lacking in the messaged "your attractions may not change") is that as they follow their deeper values rather than their current feelings, they do so with an eye for how their gifts and passions might develop along a trajectory of faithfulness and purpose.[81]

We are getting at the importance of vocation, although I hesitate to use the word. I am reluctant in part because it is a word that is so foreign to our ears, particularly the ears of evangelical Christians. What cannot be experienced as vocational is the "No" that gay Christians currently hear in the discussions about how they ought to live their lives. This is keeping with Eve Tushnet's observation:

> Right now gay teens hear a robust "Yes!" from the mainstream media and gay culture. From the Church, they hear only a "No." And you can't have a vocation of not-gay-marrying and not-having-sex. You can't have a vocation of No.[82]

In her reflections on vocation, Tushnet shares, "you *don't* always choose what God is asking of you, and it's rare that the greatest sacrifices in your life are the ones you chose entirely freely."[83]

ON BEING COUNTER-CULTURAL

I appreciate what my pastor has said from the pulpit about our decisions in the area of sexuality and sexual behavior. Essentially it is this: *What you do with your sexuality is one of the most important testimonies you give to an unbelieving world.*

When we do other good deeds in service of humanity and of the Kingdom, people in our culture today appreciate those acts and respect us. When Christians bring clean water to a remote village in Africa, people in our culture respect us. When Christians provide shelter to those in the inner city who do not have adequate housing, people appreciate what we are doing. When we tutor children at risk for illiteracy, people in our society will stand and applaud.

But when Christians live out our faith in the decisions we make in our sexuality and sexual behavior, it is truly counter-cultural. As a youth pastor, if you want to talk with your teens about living a counter-cultural life, helping them see the choices they make in this area—whether they are sexual minorities or not—is a witness to a culture that is increasingly unfamiliar with why Christians choose to live as they do.

How is a vocational understanding of sexuality cultivated? How is this kind of faithfulness to a vision for living fostered in a person? Faithfulness is not fostered by promising heterosexuality. Faithfulness is fostered by recognizing how God has provided for that person, others in the Christian community, others throughout Christian history, and so on. It is the provision and the trust found in God as the one who made me and can use me as I am to further his purposes for this world.

There are also very practical aspects of a vocational understanding and a stewardship view of sexuality.[84] Parents and youth pastors can aid teens in learning and developing specific skills, such as basic relationship skills, decision-making, delayed gratification, assertiveness, and self-control. Of course, how we grow in and display these skills is going to be tied to a young person's needs. These include a need for identity and community, as we have discussed, but also a need to be in meaningful relationships in which they are valued, as well as a need to know they are doing things that are significant; that what they do matters. This is related to the larger narrative we are "storying" about who we are as believers—that we are part of a community that is doing something that is of significance in the world today.

This is when we can discuss values. To meet these kinds of needs (for meaningful relationships and significance), young people will watch the steps taken by their parents and those in ministry and other leadership positions. We communicate the values we want our youth to "catch" in the choices we make. We can say we value meaningful relationships, but if we choose to engage in other activities that compete with the kind of intimacy we say we value, our youth will emulate what we are doing rather than what we are saying.

There are important beliefs that are up for grabs in our culture today but that are important for the Christian. These are contrasted in Figure 12 with unhelpful thoughts that can often be seen in the Christian community.

CONCLUSION

My hope is that this book will help you to lay a foundation for taking your youth ministry in a different direction. Hopefully, you have expanded your understanding of the conflict young people experience between their sexual identity and religious identity. That conflict, coupled with the normal developmental process of identity formation and answering fundamental questions about identity and community, sets the stage for how to make meaning out of experiences of same-sex attraction. The main meaning-making structures today set up a stark contrast for youth. One the one hand, we have a very positive, affirming script from the mainstream gay community. This Gay script contrasts sharply with the shame-based messages that result from our silence and "us versus them" way of relating through the culture wars.

UNHELPFUL FOR FOSTERING VOCATION/STEWARDSHIP	HELPFUL FOR FOSTERING VOCATION/STEWARDSHIP
• I am acceptable to God only if I am good in every way. • Life should be easy, fair, and make me happy, even during the most difficult times; if it is not, then I am being punished for my weak faith. • God wants to meet my every need perfectly, so if life is tough it must be because of my sin and defective faith. • Good Christians do not feel angry, fearful, or down, nor do they feel sexual desires. • I should hide my imperfetions so I do not disgrace God.	• I am a child of God, made in God's image, and loved by God. • The goal of life is not necessarily to be happy, but to love God and to become Christ-like in the way God intended. • My sexuality and sexual experiences are not unknown to God; rather, they can be a means to serve Kingdom purposes. • God wants me to be honest about my emotions and to foster a healthy view of myself as a sexual person. • God's instruction is a trustworthy guide for living in all areas, including my sexuality.

Figure 9. *Unhelpful and Helpful Thoughts for Fostering Vocation/Stewardship*

But there is hope—realistic, biblical hope. Not a hope based on a heightened expectation of heterosexuality, although meaningful movement along a continuum may be experienced by some people. But a hope that is based on identifying meaning and purpose in our lives—of living a story in which we learn what it means to delight in the purposes of God. This involves learning what it means to walk faithfully before God. The hope we want to offer youth is based on finding their identity and community in the Body of Christ, on finding meaning and purpose in stewarding their sexuality and their vocation. And this hope is based on models that others have developed, those who are a few steps ahead of them, who have storied their lives in a way that relies on God's mercy and grace, even as they navigate sexual identity.

It is a hope that begins with compassion.

CHECK YOUR COMPASS

1. How would you describe the benefits and draw-backs to each of the three approaches to ministry described in this chapter? How might the ministry approaches be related to one another?

2. How would you like these ministry approaches to inform your work with youth who are navigating sexual-identity concerns?

3. Where would you like your teaching and ministry to "land" as it pertains to hope?

4. What are some practical ways you could promote to your youth the idea of stewarding our sexuality? How about the vocational aspect?

ENDNOTES

1. "Side B" gay Christians are contrasted with "Side A" gay Christians, and this language comes from the Gay Christian Network, which was originally established as a forum for dialogue. Side A refers to those who have concluded that same-sex behavior and relationships are morally permissible, while Side B refers to those who have concluded that such relationships are not.

2. The phrase "convicted civility" comes from Richard Mouw, former president of Fuller Theological Seminary. I recently spoke at Fuller and had the opportunity to talk with Mouw at length. He credited Martin Marty for the phrase. Its origin was tied to the observation that we have far too many Christians who are strong on convictions but do not represent Christ in a way that is respectful of others. At the same time, we have Christians who are so concerned not to offend anyone that it is hard to know what they hold convictions about. So the phrase "convicted civility" reflects a balance between holding convictions as a Christian and communicating those convictions with civility.

3. Sexual identity as the act of labeling oneself based upon one's sexual preferences will come across as a rather truncated vision of identity to some people. Discussion among Christians of sexual identity will also reference a broader understanding of identity, and it will have to take into account the historical and cultural

context within which identity is formed. As Ron Belgau has shared, few people have historically had the opportunity to explore their identity in the way many do today, and much of the literature from contemporary psychology, including studies I cite throughout this book, assume that identity formation is a process by which an individual's (rather autonomous) decisions lead to the construction of an identity "for themselves." As Christians delve into these topics, our understanding of how both our sexual identity and our broader identity are constructed will inform our approach to topics such as vocation. See Ron Belgau, "Toward new models for faithful pastoral initiatives with gay and lesbian persons," unpublished manuscript, reviewed April 2, 2013.

4. I would like to thank Karen Keen (personal communication, March 23, 2013) for helping me make the distinction between Gay (noun) and gay (adjective) and for sharing some of the benefits people have found in the distinction. For two contrasting accounts on the use of "gay Christian," see Joshua Gonnerman, "Why I Call Myself A Gay Christian," and Daniel Mattson's, "Why I Don't Call Myself a Gay Christian," *First Things*, May 23, 2012.

5. Karen Keen (personal communication, March 23, 2013).

6. Andrew Marin, *Love is an Orientation*. Downers Grove, IL: InterVarsity Press.

7. Mark A. Yarhouse, Erica S. N. Tan, & Lisa M. Pawlowski, "Sexual identity development and synthesis among LGB-identified and LGB-dis-identified persons." *Journal of Psychology and Theology, 33* (1), p. 8.

8. *Childhood and Society* (2nd ed.) (1963), New York: Norton.

9. *Theories of developmental psychology* (2nd edition). New York: W.H. Freeman & Company, p. 187.

10. Jeffrey Arnett explains that while identity formation may begin in adolescence, it "intensifies in emerging adulthood," which he recognizes as a time after adolescence and before young adulthood. Of love in adolescence, he writes that the question is "Who would I enjoy being with, here and now?" while in emerging adulthood the question is "What kind of person am I, and what kind of person would suit me best as a partner through life?" Jeffrey Jensen Arnett,

Emerging Adulthood: The Winding Road from the Late Teens through the Twenties. New York: Oxford University Press, 2004, p. 9.

11. James E. Marcia, Development and Validation of Ego Identity Status, *Journal of Personality and Social Psychology,* 3 (1966), pp. 551-558.

12. This idea of a sexual identity dilemma is captured well in Wolkomir's ethnographic study comparing Gay Christians in the Metropolitan Community Church and ex-gay individuals who were participating in Exodus affiliated ministries, which announced in June 2013 that it is shutting down operations. See Michelle Wolkomir, *Be Not Deceived: The Sacred and Sexual Struggles of Gay and Ex-Gay Christian Men.* New Jersey: Rutgers University Press, 2006, pp. 39-53.

13. *Ibid.*, p. 47.

14. Ritch C. Savin-Williams and Lisa M. Diamond (2000). "Sexual identity trajectories among sexual minority youths: Gender comparisons." *Archives of Sexual Behavior, 29* (6), 607-627; Ritch C. Savin-Williams & Kenneth M. Cohen (2004). "Homoerotic development during childhood and adolescence." In Milton Diamond and Alayne Yates (Eds.), *Child and Adolescent Psychiatric Clinics of North America: Sex and Gender* (pp. 529-550). Philadelphia, PA: Saunders.

15. The ranges are from two studies: Stephen P. Stratton, Janet B. Dean, Mark A. Yarhouse, & Michael Lastoria, Sexual Minorities in Faith-Based Higher Education: A National Survey of Attitudes, Milestones, Identity, and Religiosity. *Journal of Psychology and Theology*, 2013, pp. 3-23; Mark A. Yarhouse, Stephen P. Stratton, Janet B. Dean & Heather L. Brooke (2009), Listening to sexual minorities on Christian college campuses. *Journal of Psychology and Theology, 37* (2), 96-113. We report similar findings for milestone events in the 2009 study of Christian sexual minorities: 28.7% engaged in SSB, 13.9% adopted a Gay identity, and 20% reported an ongoing same-sex relationship.

16. Ritch C. Savin-Williams and Lisa M. Diamond (2000). Sexual identity trajectories among sexual minority youths: Gender comparisons. *Archives of Sexual Behavior, 29* (6), 607-627.

17. The authors note that these numbers are lower than is often reported (which is closer to between ages 9-11 for first same-sex attractions), and that it may be due to the unique wording in their study: "Describe your first memories of being attracted to girls/ boys. How old were you and what specifically do you remember? You need not have interpreted the attractions as sexual in nature *at that time*. How far back can you recall such an experience?" Ritch C. Savin-Williams and Lisa M. Diamond (2000). Sexual identity trajectories among sexual minority youths: Gender comparisons. *Archives of Sexual Behavior, 29* (6), p. 615.

18. The researchers did not ask about this in their study; however, other studies of males have put this at about age 18. See E. M. Dube, & R. C. Savin-Williams, Sexual identity development among ethnic sexual minority male youths. *Developmental Psychology, 35*, 1389-1399.

19. Ritch C. Savin-Williams and Lisa M. Diamond (2000). "Sexual identity trajectories among sexual minority youths: Gender comparisons." *Archives of Sexual Behavior, 29* (6), p. 621.

20. *Ibid.*, pp. 621-622.

21. Stephen P. Stratton, Janet B. Dean, Mark A. Yarhouse, & Michael Lastoria, "Sexual Minorities in Faith-Based Higher Education: A National Survey of Attitudes, Milestones, Identity, and Religiosity." *Journal of Psychology and Theology*, 2013, pp. 3-23.

22. Mark A. Yarhouse, Stephen P. Stratton, Janet B. Dean & Heather L. Brooke (2009), "Listening to sexual minorities on Christian college campuses." *Journal of Psychology and Theology, 37* (2), 96-113. In this study the average age of various milestone events were as follows: awareness of same-sex feelings (12.96 years old); same-sex sexual behavior to orgasm (16.42); initial attribution that they were gay (17.22); labeling as gay (17.93); and first same-sex relationship (18.19).

23. Mark A. Yarhouse, Heather L. Brooke, Paula Pisano & Erica S. N. Tan, "Project Inner Compass: Young adults experiencing sexual identity confusion," *Journal of Psychology and Christianity, 24* (4), p. 353.

24. Mark A. Yarhouse, Heather L. Brooke, Paula Pisano & Erica S. N.

Tan, "Project Inner Compass: Young adults experiencing sexual identity confusion." *Journal of Psychology and Christianity,* 24 (4), p. 353.

25. Mark A. Yarhouse, Heather L. Brooke, Paula Pisano & Erica S. N. Tan, "Project Inner Compass: Young adults experiencing sexual identity confusion." *Journal of Psychology and Christianity,* 24 (4), p. 357.

26. P. J. Egan, M. S. Edelman, & K. Sherrill, *Findings from the Hunter College Poll of Lesbians, Gays, and Bisexuals: New Discoveries about Identity, Political Attitudes, and Civic Engagement* (New York: The City University of New York, 2008).

27. Lisa M. Diamond, *Sexual Fluidity: Understanding Women's Love and Desire,* 2006. Cambridge, MA: Harvard University Press, pp. 91ff.

28. Mark A. Yarhouse and Erica S. N. Tan (2004), *Sexual identity synthesis: Attributions, meaning-making and the search for congruence.* Lanham, MD: University Press of America, pp. 105-132.

29. For example, Wesley Hill wrote about this decision: ". . . I use 'same-sex attraction,' 'homosexual desires,' 'homosexuality,' and related terms interchangeably. Likewise, I've used a variety of designations for gay and lesbian people. Instead of sticking to one term, such as 'homosexual Christian,' I also refer to myself as a 'gay Christian' or 'a Christian who experiences homosexual desires.' These phrases are all synonymous for me, and though they are open to misunderstanding, in my judgment the gains in using them outweigh the potential hazards. None of them should be taken necessarily to imply homosexual practice; in each case I am most often placing the emphasis on the subject's sexual orientation and not the corresponding behavior." Wesley Hill, *Washed and Waiting.* Grand Rapids, MI: Zondervan, 2010, p. 21.

30. Mark A. Yarhouse and Erica S. N. Tan (2004), *Sexual identity synthesis: Attributions, meaning-making and the search for congruence.* Lanham, MD: University Press of America, p. 116.

31. See Ritch C. Savin-Williams and Lisa M. Diamond (2000), "Sexual identity trajectories among sexual minority youths: Gender comparisons." *Archives of Sexual Behavior,* 29 (6), pp. 615-622.

32. Jeffrey Jensen Arnett, *Emerging Adulthood: The Winding Road from*

the Late Teens through the Twenties. New York: Oxford University Press, 2004, p. 167.

33. Mark A. Yarhouse, *Homosexuality and the Christian: A Guide for Parents, Pastors and Friends.* Bethany House, 2010.

34. Mark A. Yarhouse and Erica S. N. Tan (2004), *Sexual identity synthesis: Attributions, meaning-making and the search for congruence.* Lanham, MD: University Press of America, p. 112.

35. *Ibid.*, p. 113.

36. Mark A. Yarhouse, Erica S. N. Tan, & Lisa M. Pawlowski, "Sexual identity development and synthesis among LGB-identified and LGB-dis-identified persons." *Journal of Psychology and Theology,* *33* (1), p. 11.

37. Mark A. Yarhouse, Heather L. Brooke, Paula Pisano & Erica S. N. Tan, "Project Inner Compass: Young adults experiencing sexual identity confusion," *Journal of Psychology and Christianity,* *24* (4), p. 358.

38. Veronica R. F. Johnson and Mark A. Yarhouse, "Shame in sexual minorities: Stigma, internal cognitions, and counseling considerations." *Counseling and Values, 85*, p. 85.

39. *Ibid.*, p. 85.

40. *Ibid.*, p. 87.

41. Mark A. Yarhouse, Heather L. Brooke, Paula Pisano & Erica S. N. Tan, "Project Inner Compass: Young adults experiencing sexual identity confusion," *Journal of Psychology and Christianity,* *24* (4), p. 358.

42. Mark A. Yarhouse, Erica S. N. Tan, & Lisa M. Pawlowski, "Sexual identity development and synthesis among LGB-identified and LGB-dis-identified persons." *Journal of Psychology and Theology,* *33* (1), p. 11.

43. See Elizabeth C. Suarez and Mark A. Yarhouse, "The impact of sexual abuse on sexual identity." In Andrew J. Schmutzer (Ed.), *The Long Journey Home: Understanding and Ministering to the Sexually Abused* (pp. 90-101). Eugene, OR: Wipf & Stock.

44. Mark A. Yarhouse (2010), *Homosexuality and the Christian: A guide for parents, pastors and friends.* Minneapolis, MN: Bethany House, pp. 57-80.

45. G. Remafedi, M. Resnick, R. Blum, & L. Harris, "Demography of Sexual Orientation in Adolescents." *Pediatrics*, 1992, 89 (4), 714-721.

46. The language of "Side A" and "Side B" gay Christians comes from the Gay Christian Network, which is run by Justin Lee, a Side A Christian who envisioned it to be a forum for dialogue between those who are gay and Christian and view same-sex behavior and relationships as morally permissible (Side A) and those who do not (Side B).

47. Ritch C. Savin-Williams & Geoffrey L. Ream, "Prevalence and Stability of Sexual Orientation Components During Adolescence and Young Adulthood." *Archives of Sexual Behavior* (2007), *36*, pp. 385-394.

48. The 2002 National Survey of Family Growth, for example, found that 4.3% of males and 10.7% of females between the ages of 15-19 reported engaging in same-sex behavior. However, in this study, the question asked of boys was specific to oral and anal sex, while the question asked of females asked about "any sexual behavior of any kind," which likely contributed to a much higher percentage (or, conversely, the wording for the males contributed to a much lower percentage among adolescent males). See Mark D. Regnerus, *Forbidden Fruit: Sex & Religion in the Lives of American Teenagers.* New York, Oxford University Press (2007), p. 260.

49. Interestingly, in the third wave of the Add Health study, at age 22, 5.6% of males and 14.5% of females indicated that they were *not exclusively heterosexual*. Even in this case, most of the teens who did not say they were exclusively heterosexual did not identify themselves as gay/bisexual but as "mostly heterosexual." See Savin-Williams & Ream, p. 388.

50. Same-sex attraction and behavior were less stable over time than opposite-sex attraction and behavior. In other words, teens who reported any same-sex attraction or behavior here tended to "migrate" toward heterosexuality over time. Put differently, there was more sexual stability reported by adolescents who initially reported opposite-sex attraction or behavior than adolescents who initially reported same-sex or both same- and opposite-sex

attraction or behavior. Adolescents who reported same-sex behavior and both same- and opposite-sex behavior at ages 16 and 17 were more likely to engage in exclusive opposite-sex behavior at age 22 (to "migrate" toward heterosexuality) than those adolescents who had reported opposite-sex behavior at 16 or 17 were to move toward same-sex or same- and opposite-sex behavior at 22. Some teens did migrate in the other direction as well. *Ibid.*, pp. 389, 393.

51. The problem with this line of thinking is that it assumes an essentialist understanding of sexual orientation. From this point of view, sexual orientation is a real, stable, enduring, and essential aspect of a person, something that exists across all cultures and throughout history. This view lends itself to more rigid categorization. In contrast, social constructivism asserts that sexual orientation is a social construct, that heterosexuality and homosexuality are not real, enduring, stable aspects of our sexuality but rather are linguistic constructs for naming sexual preferences. While a youth pastor need not land in one particular view of sexual orientation, it is wise to consider how rigid categorization of Gay or 100% heterosexual might be unhelpful and even contribute to questioning and confusion for some teens.

52. Mark A. Yarhouse, Heather L. Brooke, Paula Pisano & Erica S. N. Tan, "Project Inner Compass: Young adults experiencing sexual identity confusion." *Journal of Psychology and Christianity, 24* (4), p. 356.

53. Thank you to Barrett McRay for his reflections on this point.

54. *Ibid.*, p. 355.

55. *Ibid.*, p. 355.

56. *Ibid.*, p. 356.

57. *Ibid.*, p. 355.

58. Veronica R. F. Johnson and Mark A. Yarhouse, "Shame in sexual minorities: Stigma, internal cognitions, and counseling considerations." *Counseling and Values, 85*, p. 87.

59. Mark A. Yarhouse, Heather L. Brooke, Paula Pisano & Erica S. N. Tan, "Project Inner Compass: Young adults experiencing sexual identity confusion," *Journal of Psychology and Christianity, 24* (4), p. 358.

60. Veronica R. F. Johnson and Mark A. Yarhouse, "Shame in sexual

minorities: Stigma, internal cognitions, and counseling considerations." *Counseling and Values, 85*, p. 87.

61. Steve Gerali, *The Struggle*, 2003, Colorado Springs: NavPress, p. 179. One consideration given our topic of sexual identity is that when many Christian ministers discuss masturbation, they do so with reference to maintaining purity for a teenager's eventual spouse. This approach falls short of speaking into the lives of many heterosexual teens who will remain single, as well as the experiences of sexual minorities. Youth pastors will need to reflect on a broader set of considerations as they discuss this topic with adolescents today, and I think Gerali's book provides a helpful framework for teaching and discussion. If a teen you are ministering to is also struggling with pornography, you might consider the use of an app like Private Integrity, which is something I recently helped develop. The functionality of that app is also available online at www.privateintegrity.org.

62. Veronica Johnson (2009), *Reducing shame: A resource for Christians who experience same-sex attractions*. Available from the author.

63. Terry D. Cooper, *Making Judgments without Being Judgmental*. Downers Grove, IL: InterVarsity Press, 2006, p. 121.

64. Joyce J. Penner and Clifford L. Penner (2005), *Counseling for Sexual Disorders*. Dallas, TX: Word, pp. 11-22.

65. *Ibid.*, p. 21.

66. The Restored Hope Network is an example of this ministry focus. This is a relatively new network of ministries that came about after a falling out with Exodus International, which has historically been the flagship ministry for people who experience unwanted same-sex attractions. Exodus announced in June 2013 that it is shutting down operations.

67. Many of the former Exodus International affiliates were in this area, although some might also feel more comfortable in the hope for change emphasis discussed above. I suspect that the split that occurred with the Restored Hope Network led away from Exodus many ministries that would be more comfortable with a "hope for change" model. Exodus announced in June 2013 that it is shutting down operations.

68. http://spiritualfriendship.org/

69. Thank you to Julie Rodgers for helping me think through this point. See also Eve Tushnet's observation on this matter—that it is "very easy for teenagers of any sexual orientation to have unrealistic romantic ideas in which marriage solves the problem of the self, grants us our 'soulmate' and ends our loneliness forever." http://www.theamericanconservative.com/the-botany-club-gay-kids-in-catholic-schools/

70. Karen Keen, personal communication, March 21, 2013.

71. Wesley Hill, *Washed and Waiting*. Grand Rapids, MI: Zondervan.

72. http://www.firstthings.com/blogs/firstthoughts/2013/02/01/once-more-on-the-label-gay-christian/, downloaded April 12, 2013.

73. Mark A. Yarhouse, Erica S. N. Tan, & Lisa M. Pawlowski, "Sexual identity development and synthesis among LGB-identified and LGB-dis-identified persons." *Journal of Psychology and Theology, 33* (1), p. 8.

74. Mark A. Yarhouse and Erica S. N. Tan (2004), *Sexual identity synthesis: Attributions, meaning-making and the search for congruence.* Lanham, MD: University Press of America, p. 109.

75. *Ibid.*, p. 113.

76. *Ibid.*, p. 113.

77. Eugene Peterson, *A long obedience in the same direction*. Downers Grove, IL: InterVarsity Press, 1980, p. 169.

78. *Ibid.*, p. 8.

79. A special thank you to Liam Coventry for sharing how he establishes an atmosphere of grace in his youth group.

80. Eve Tushnet, downloaded April 10, 2013: http://www.theamericanconservative.com/the-botany-club-gay-kids-in-catholic-schools/

81. Thank you again to Julie Rodgers for her thoughts on this when she reviewed an earlier version of this chapter.

82. Eve Tushnet, downloaded April 10, 2013 http://www.theamericanconservative.com/the-botany-club-gay-kids-in-catholic-schools/

This quote reminds me of an exchange I had with an acquaintance of mine. She is a lesbian psychologist who reviewed a study

I had conducted of Christians who identified as Gay and Christian sexual minorities who did not. She asked, "How can people form an identity with a negative? Is that a sustainable identity? What is the psychological impact of that over time?" These are important questions about identity, and we are extending that into the important area of vocation, as I believe they are connected.

83. This is in reference to the criticism often raised in discussions in a Catholic context that priests are called to a life of celibacy, whereas gay and lesbian persons are told they are obligated to follow standards to which they have not been called.

84. I am drawing here on the discussion by Stanton and Brenna Jones on character featured in *How and When to Tell Your Kids about Sex* (2nd ed.). Colorado Springs, CO: NavPress, 2007. The figure on unhelpful and helpful thoughts is also adapted from Jones and Jones.

Share Your Thoughts

With the Author: Your comments will be forwarded to the author when you send them to *zauthor@zondervan.com*.

With Zondervan: Submit your review of this book by writing to *zreview@zondervan.com*.

Free Online Resources at

www.zondervan.com

Daily Bible Verses and Devotions: Enrich your life with daily Bible verses or devotions that help you start every morning focused on God. Visit www.zondervan.com/newsletters.

Free Email Publications: Sign up for newsletters on Christian living, academic resources, church ministry, fiction, children's resources, and more. Visit www.zondervan.com/newsletters.

Zondervan Bible Search: Find and compare Bible passages in a variety of translations at www.zondervanbiblesearch.com.

Other Benefits: Register to receive online benefits like coupons and special offers, or to participate in research.